Insights on Retirement:

THE WONDER YEARS OF YOUR LIFE

Jay Hettiarachchy

This work is dedicated to my wife Professor Navam Hettiarachchy, Ph.D., and two sons Gnanin L. Hettiarachchy, M.D., and Rukmin R. Hettiarachchy, M.D., who are the three most precious persons in my life

Preface

Retirement from work has become a reality today. It has also become affordable to most workers and not just an unfulfilled dream people have anymore. However, most often negative feelings and attitudes towards retirement continue to affect working people as well as those who are ready to retire from work and relax during their golden years of life. One of the main objectives of this book is to make valuable observations regarding such negative opinions and mind-sets that are mostly unfounded preventing people from entering the world of retirement where they could spend the remaining years of their life comfortably, happily, and free.

Undoubtedly, the work phase of an individual's life gives her/him the opportunity of achieving the full potential of life by enabling them to offer their talents and abilities as a service for which they are compensated. Also it is true that the self-worth, self-esteem, and the social status of a person in the society mostly depend on the type of work that s/he does. These reasons may possibly contribute to certain negative feelings, reluctance, and/or possible postponement of retirement by some workers who continue to work even beyond their retirement age. Nevertheless retirement is a choice available to most workers to relax and enjoy a carefree life.

The retirement phase in life of a person is to enjoy life free from any obligations or other limitations that most people encounter during the time when they build their careers continuously setting their career goals. It is also a time they have for themselves rather than for others or for a service they provide for others. True retirement is not about having to enter a second phase of work life as most people would think. It is about a second life in which one could virtually do the things that s/he wanted to do in life and never had the time to spend or the opportunity for doing it.

The insights given at the end of each chapter are stepping stones meant to dispel the negative mental attitudes and prejudices held by some workers in general regarding retirement from work. They provide valuable ideas for formulating a plan for the retirement phase of life from the very beginning to the end of any career most people engage in, during the most productive years of their life. The insights reveal that a systematic plan for retirement is as important for every worker as a career plan they do develop throughout their working years.

Retirement certainly is an entitlement of people who have done a lifetime of hard work. They have a right to enjoy their life to the fullest extent by being happy, contented, and free during their final stage of life. This book is an attempt to address some of the most important aspects of the retirement phase of life, the importance of which is somewhat marginalized by the currently held social attitudes and prejudices.

I wish to thank my wife Navam Hettiarachchy and brother Lalith Hettiarachchy for proof reading, and giving me valuable suggestions to improve the quality of this book.

I hope you enjoy this book as much as I enjoyed writing it.

Jay Hettiarachchy, Professor Emeritus
(Ferris State University, Big Rapids, Michigan)
2989 E. Setter Street, Fayetteville, AR 72701.

Forward

Unlike in the past, retirement has become an affordable way of life for most people in almost every country and nation in the world today. Advances in medical sciences and pharmaceutical research, have enabled most people to live a longer life. For these reasons, I found this work not only timely and relevant providing very valuable information and insights from an entirely different perspective regarding one's retirement phase of life, but also a very useful reference book in the hands of any working person including those who are already retired. As a semi-retired person, I can certainly appreciate and relate to the relevancy of the views that the author holds and presents as food for thought for a working person regarding retirement and the importance of planning for retirement systematically discussed throughout the entire book.

Most often employed people do postpone thinking about retirement until the day they retire. The author however, clearly shows in his writings that whether a person is employed in public service, a private enterprise, or is self-employed, ultimately s/he has to face the reality of retirement from work and therefore it is far better to plan for one's retirement early in life than late or not at all. The same principle applies to non-working folks as well – the category of people, mostly women who do part-time work among all other tasks that they perform, including and not limited to, household activities as well as the rearing and caring of young children. They too are certainly entitled to retire from such work and enjoy a phase of life of their own, in retirement, at least during the golden years of their life.

The author brings into clear focus that we need to "live" our life, and therefore the main purpose of retirement is to relax and enjoy every moment of the remaining life of a person after having worked for at least two thirds of her/his life. He also reinforces the overall importance of planning for retirement by people irrespective of their social, cultural, religious backgrounds and affiliations and their beliefs on life after death that may to a great extent have a bearing on their views and beliefs of temporal life versus after-life expectations.

This book has a wealth of information presented very objectively and lucidly. Undoubtedly, some people tend to neglect, overlook, or sometimes even refuse to accept certain basic facts of life. As an example, in the chapter on Sunset Years (Chapter 9), the author points out that the average person who tends to care about her/his body fails to recognize the importance of the mind that too is susceptible to sickness as much as the body. This is supported by research as well. The author has made an attempt in this chapter to show how a proper understanding of the workings of our mind and mental attitudes could contribute significantly in improving our retirement life.

Presumably, the vast majority of present-day retirees are married people sharing their life with their spouses in their retirement years while the number of people living single and therefore spending their retirement life single, seems to be on the rise. Unlike in the case of single retirees, the death of a soul-partner is a challenge that married retirees have to invariably face some day. The last chapter addresses this issue of handling it by some who are less-well or unprepared for it, rather poorly. It is very natural that most people, who lose the function of their senses in their old age, tend to get frustrated, irritated, and at times behave very irrationally. Being prepared to deal with such life events by all parties concerned in a family, is therefore of utmost importance as we do go through the inevitable life changes and events, either by ourselves or by those who we do love and care for in our life.

The author also discusses in some detail the various avenues and opportunities that are available to retirees to spend the remaining years of their life enjoyably as the function of caring for the elderly by the children is gradually diminishing due to their other pressing needs and commitments they have in the present day societies. The book contains a wealth of information for anybody, working, non-working, near retirement or retired.

Lalith Hettiarachchy
Retired from Sri Lankan Administrative Service
(Local and Foreign Service),
Currently serving as the Director of Projects of
Navaloka Construction in Colombo, Sri Lanka.

Contents

Chapter One

Why Not Retire?

Retirement is a state of mind

People today live longer, healthier lives, and they have more opportunities and resources to comfortably live at least ¼ th of their life in retirement. As the agrarian economy was replaced by the industrial and informational economies, white-collar jobs with high income also rose. The result of this economy boost was obvious. People living a longer life probably had saved more money than their predecessors, they have more time to live, more opportunities and choices they could make that their forefathers could not even dream of during their lifetime. Retirement that was probably unthinkable by the workers who lived and worked during the 19th and 20th centuries has now become a reality for most working people in the developed parts of the world. In the United States itself approximately seventy six million baby boomers were born between 1946 and 1964 (http://en.wikipedia.org/wiki/Baby_boomers) who would be retiring or thinking of retiring from work at this time. This book is intended for not only those who have reached the threshold of retirement, especially those who belong to the baby boomer generation, but also for every working person who would eventually have a choice to retire from work, if they do want to eventually retire. It is also for those who have a hard time making the decision to retire from work that provides them with a sense of self-worthiness that they mostly need for their continued success at work and life, in general.

Many people retire from work due to various reasons, most importantly poor health. Another important reason is that they want to do something that they really wanted to do but could not afford the time for doing it during the employment phase of life. But there are other people who do not want to retire from work even after 70 years of age. This is mainly because they enjoy their work that gives them energy, satisfaction and happiness in life; they are passionate about what they accomplish at work. Such people have a burning desire to make a difference and a positive impact on other people's life and are willing to put off retirement as long as they could.

There is another category of people however, who have to go for work to make a living. They have to make money to pay for their daily expenses, car liens, house mortgages, and most other financial bill payments including credit card bills they have to settle at the end of each and every month. Some of them have children to feed and clothe and they worry about their own life and their children's life. Retirement from work may not be an option for this category of people. They will look for even part-time work if they are laid off from work due to job performance related, or other issues at work. If this category of people had the foresight to think ahead of their retirement and made at least small amounts of savings on a regular basis, such savings could help them enormously during the time when they are unable to work anymore.

A personal note by the author on retirement:

Knowing both the pros and cons of retirement and having made a decision over three years after reading over 10 books written by researchers and writers on retirement, a list of which is given at the end of this book, the author gave two years of notice to his employer of his plans to retire. Most of the time, employers like it when someone who holds a senior position in an institution wants to retire. This is because they could probably hire two young people or temporary hands to fill the vacancy for the salary they paid for one senior retiree.

Also, the realization that there are many other things that people could or should do besides working, at least during the time when they have the financial resources and time to do such things, contributed to my decision to retire. Moreover, retirement from work provides the necessary freedom as well as the opportunity for a person to do the things s/he is passionate about. This made me think, that we should redefine the word "work" at least to suit the ideal life of a retired person. The dictionary meaning of the term "work" is:

1) a job or activity that you do regularly in order to earn money 2) the place where you do your work 3) the things that you do especially as part of your job (Source: http://www.merriam-webster.com/dictionary/work). As we see, work as an employment or profession may mean to most working people an opportunity to do certain things that in turn pays them a remuneration. As shown earlier, some people may not be terribly enthusiastic about the work they do as others who are passionate about what they do in their work places. The "work" as far as a retiree is concerned may not necessarily be associated with earning money. Therefore, "the work that a retiree may be engaged in, would be the result of an insatiable passion s/he may have had for doing certain thing/s that s/he wanted to do in life, but never had the time and opportunity to engage in it."

Yes, there is a time to work, as much as there is a time to be a student, a married person, a working person, or a retired person. Mixing up these stages of life can cause complications to many people. It can be unfortunate if people do not devote the time to study and learn how to manage their life so that they could live comfortably during each stage of their life. Admittedly, we cannot plan our life so perfectly that everything happens according to our wishes, plans and expectations. However, most people can live a better life and make better decisions and choices about their life by having a proper plan. Planning has advantages over non-planning or poor planning. It goes without saying that having a plan could help achieve our goals better than not having a plan at all. Planning for rretirement works the same way. One has to have a proper plan for retirement. If one does not study it, communicate about it, and plan for it, one will wake up in retirement without having planned for it, and this an uncomfortable place to spend one's life in retirement.

Insight # 1
Work and Retirement are mutually exclusive.

If we try to combine the work phase and retirement phase of life as some people do, we will most probably be burning the candle at both ends. Retiring is a state of mind that allows a working person to rise above work-life and ambitions at work including letting go of such common human aspirations that need to be left behind by the retiree at the work-place that s/he leaves behind. Continuing to miss the work-world that a retiree leaves behind even after her/his retirement will therefore have a tendency to take away the limited time a retiree may have to enjoy the retirement benefits to the fullest extent.

Given below are two postings that I copied from Facebook that I found relevant to the theme of this chapter:

Professor Doug Haneline on 1/13/2014

"I was always an early bird as a teacher, requesting 8 am classes. So were I still working, I would be in my office and the copy room right now, attending to the small details that assure a smooth launch to the semester. I miss seeing my colleagues and sharing stories of Christmas break, and I miss that peculiar anticipation one feels in the onset of the great adventure of learning. But I don't miss the feeling of being rushed, the news of yet another meeting, or whining students with excuses I've heard before. I still like helping people with their writing, so my nine weekly hours in the

Writing Center are enjoyable. But I am enjoying sleeping late, planning my travels, thinking about my garden and landscaping, reading, volunteering, and generally hanging out. Retirement was the right choice".

Professor <u>Richard Hewer</u>
<u>January 17</u>, 2014

"Great day teaching yesterday. Left at 9:00 and got home at 10:00. Did 8 hours of lecturing in between and really enjoyed doing the lectures. Most hours I have ever lectured in a day and one of the most enjoyable days lecturing. Why retire?"

Chapter Two

The Rationale for Retirement

To be trapped in a dream is equally bad as to be trapped in reality

If you picked up this book to read, most probably you worked most of your productive life and you are thinking of retiring or you are already a retired person. As pointed out in the previous chapter, retirement was not possible during the previous generations in most countries unlike today when a large number of people who had a productive work-life, a desire to retire, and saved sufficient money for a happy retirement, have the opportunity to spend the rest of their life relaxed in their golden years of life. However, there are some people in the work-world even today who are unaware that the best time to think about and plan for retirement is the time when they are young and at the prime time of their life, getting ready to begin their careers. If you belong to this category and did not think about retirement until now, hopefully you have time to do so and do some catching up and be very happy about the decision that you make now. Even if you are already retired, you may find some useful hints and ideas you could be taking away with you after reading this chapter which is written to benefit almost everyone about the concept of retirement that has become a reality for almost every worker who had a productive work life.

It is a common saying, "when your kids leave home for good and the dog dies and you are tired of working for others, it is time for you to retire". Perhaps, all these may not happen simultaneously for some folks. Some may not even have had dogs during their entire life; some folks may not even have had kids to leave home. You get the idea. Those who raised kids and had dogs do not have a reason to work and earn money to feed them and support them anymore at some point in their life, sooner or later. Therefore why not do something that you have always been passionate about doing and have been waiting all your life to do rather than doing something to make extra money to add to your savings you already have, that may most probably outlast you? After all there is no reason now to support the kids and the dogs like during the time when they needed you most, and depended on you and were a part of your family.

Some hard truths about retirement readiness:

Most educated people make better decisions and life choices regarding life than those who were not as fortunate to have learned the basic tools for pursuing and furthering their education. Also, most educated people live longer, healthier and a comparatively better life than those who were not fortunate enough to learn at least the basic educational tools needed in life. This is true of the retirement life of people as well. Most educated people, use their common sense and education to work for them to save some of their earnings for a rainy day. Those who do not save and plan for retirement can experience limited alternatives and may have to keep working even when they are very old or have to depend on their relatives or the government welfare for their daily living. Not having enough resources to support themselves at retirement is a hard truth that some people living and face even in the 21st century. This is harder when people reach advanced age and are most probably unable to work for a living. This is a lesson that young people who are just beginning to work for others should learn from those who have spent an entire life time without saving for their retirement. Choosing an employer that systematically contributes to retirement benefits of their employees is therefore an important decision most workers need to make at the beginning of their career.

Those who saved money during their prime time of life also know that money grows when money is sensibly invested. If one is not interested in managing her/his investments during retirement, there are many reliable investment firms that will manage money during their retirement years for a fee/commission. You could obtain those services if you have saved a substantial amount of money that is worth being managed by such professional management companies. However, it is likely that such companies may provide financial service most probably to people who have saved at least a minimum of $500,000 or more in liquid assets. The formula for retirement adopted by such companies, can be that a retiree needs to have saved approximately 6 times her/his last annual salary's worth, to be comfortably retiring. For example, if the last annual salary of a retiree was $80,000, s/he should have saved at least $ 480,000 in a retirement fund. This may mean that those who do not have accumulated such retirement funds have to keep working, sometimes earning a minimum wage during their advanced age. There is a very good reason therefore for young people to begin investing whatever they could afford from their salary that they earn at work on a regular basis for their retirement. This is harder on the working people of some countries where the retirement age is 55 - 65 years.

Importance of Planning and Decision Making:

Retirement is not all about money, money making and money management as discussed in most books written on retirement, although money saved contributes to a great extent during retirement years of a person. Also, having sources of money that do not dry up during your retirement years, like the money making investments that do not dry up with time would certainly help. Having sufficient property on which one does not owe any money other than the taxes to pay on them, will significantly help during the time when you live on a fixed income taken out of your savings. But, money alone cannot and may or may not make a person very happy in her/his retirement age.

It is not so much the money but a budget that would pay all the expenses through the retirement years of a retiree that matters most. If a retiree could confidently budget her/his expenses needed during her/his retirement years by projecting future needs, without having to depend on others, s/he could confidently retire. Not having to worry about day-to-day expenses and the ability to live within a budget are good enough reasons for one to retire. The key to planning such a budget is the life style that one is comfortable with and the resources that would facilitate such a life style.

Happiness and health are as important as much as money for retirement. Those people who cannot proudly say that they are going to be retired and they are happy to be retired very sincerely and honestly, should think very carefully before they make a decision to retire. This is because they may not be happy retirees; rather they will be unhappy retirees, who will be thinking constantly of their work place and wondering why they ever left their work place or worse, were laid off from work, all through their retirement years. This is because retirement has a psychological aspect to it. One has to have a retiring mind to be able to retire confidently with no regrets in order to be a happy retiree.

Most probably, you may have come across retirees who keep coming back to their previous work places due to the passion they had for work and to meet with their colleagues or provide free service to keep them occupied with the work they enjoyed. They could also be lonely and want to relate to the work-world and former co-workers that they miss after retirement. This behavior perhaps provides satisfaction to them during their retirement. Separation from work impacts different people in different ways. There is a good reason to be knowledgeable about such risks as well as opportunities that retirement presents to retirees. It is therefore most important that those who plan to retire take the time to learn about such risks and opportunities before they make their choice to retire. The hard truth however is that the time to retire will arrive sooner or later to all those who work. Those who learn about and plan for it ahead can be happy retirees.

Given below are some reasons given by workers who are thinking about retiring from work:

* To do other things
* Financial incentives
* Have enough income
* Spouse retired
* Older worker policy
* Poor health
* Did not like to work or prefer not to work
* Did not get along with boss
* Family health
* Not appreciated
* Job ended[1]

Most importantly, if a working person who had worked most of her/his productive life does not have a compelling reason to work, she has a good reason and an opportunity to retire. Some people convince themselves to keep working in order that they get tax benefits they are entitled to when they work. But one has to weigh these benefits against other risks that are more important in life for them. This applies to people who work for themselves as well as those who work for others.

A retirement card that I randomly picked up in a store stated that retirement is a "time to be with friends and family, time to relax, and do those things you really love to do, time for all of the projects you have always wanted to work on, and time to spend doing just as you please." Have you reached that time? Do not keep thinking of retiring and dreaming about it to accomplish it sometime someday. Just retire! When you are able to do so.

---

[1] The New Retirement, p. 7

Insight # 2
The best time to think about retirement is not at the end of your work-life, but at the beginning of it.

Many employers provide benefits to employees they hire. In the absence of pension plans that most workers of the past generations enjoyed, and most federal government and state government employees enjoy even to this day, some employers offer retirement plans that allow their employees to systematically contribute a certain percent of their monthly salary as tax annuities (certain percentage of their salary taken out on which tax payment is deferred, and saved in growth funds). In addition, the employer matches with a certain percentage of employee's contributions as well. Since these contributions are taken from employee salaries on pre-tax basis, it helps employees who plan their budgets ahead to reduce their annual taxes. Some employees take the time to study these employment benefits and attend seminars offered by money management companies and take the time to learn money management principles and skills. There is a good reason for new employees to study and understand such employee benefits even if they do not work for the same employer all through their work life. This is certainly an investment that every person who plans to work for others should make sooner than later. Knowledge is a powerful tool that gives power to those who have it, and use it appropriately. Employees who try to save money during their last phase of work-life realize rather late that if they had started saving in retirement funds when they were young, such savings duplicate and triplicate compounded over time during their work life. Similarly, the longer one waits to save money, the less money will be accumulated in retirement funds; if no money was saved, and every penny that one earned was spent during one's work-life, such workers will not only have any accumulated wealth to take home when they retire, but will have no dividends, which may be rare. The second insight therefore is critical when it comes to retirement. Save when you are young for your golden age which may come sooner than you expect it to come—so goes the saying "make hay while the sun shines!

Chapter Three

Retiring Mind

Work can be inspiring and/or addictive

Retired life begins when the work life ends, at least partially. Although many of the retirees would have been married with children before retirement, most other retirees may have been single, divorced, living with significant others, widowed or living with retired spouses if both husband and wife worked. This chapter is written to include all those categories of persons who are already retired, thinking of retiring in the near future, distant future, later at some point in time, sooner or later.

In reality some people who retire would not wish they had one more day to go to work unless they are workaholics or they have an obsessive compulsive tendency to work. If they knew they had one more day before they died they would have most probably planned for something they truly wanted to do rather than spending that last day at work. Unfortunately or fortunately humans do not have such a capacity to foresee future occurrences. If you ask 100 retirees what they would really want to do during their retirement, you would most probably get several different answers. You may even find people to whom this question never occurred. Also, many of those 100 people may not have wanted to do very similar things. However, the greatest advantage they have is the opportunity of choosing what they really wanted to do in their retirement life. Also, they are not doing it necessarily to make a living. They choose their time as well as break time and timeline to complete the work that would fit their own requirements.

In some parts of the world, the retirement age is 55-65 years of age in government service sector. There is the tendency in those countries for retirees to look for post-retirement-jobs such as consulting or part time jobs. Unfortunately some of these people tend to have non-working adult children who they have to support in their own homes after they retire. The mandatory retirement age at 55 years of age comes to some of those people as a wakeup call too early in their life to plan for their retirement for which they are not quite prepared. The discrepancies in retirement age become obvious when comparing the retirement age of those countries with that of the United States where in some sectors of the economy there is no mandatory age for retirement at all. Whereas most people in the United States of America retire early when they are 62 others retire at 65 or 66 years of age; those who are over 66, once they get their social security benefits are mostly ready to retire with some exceptional people who continue to work even after 70 years of age.

As mentioned earlier, increased life expectancy in the developed parts of the world has enabled working people to keep working until or after 70 years of age. Ideally, a person should be retiring one fourth of her/his life time to enjoy the full benefits of retirement and enjoy life. Unfortunately, this is not the case with many of the retirees even in the United States. Most people who retire without proper planning face such a situation at the end of their careers mainly due to postponing retirement decision until it may be too late to do so.

It is only the other day I happened to meet a retiree who told me that he took his retirement package just because it came in his way; he took his retirement because it was a good buy out deal with a lot of money in his pocket at a time when the economy of the country was going downhill and most businesses were ready to cut corners in their annual budgets. Now you see how things happen unexpectedly to people and thereby they get into a new phase of life as a matter of course. They may or may not have any idea as to how they would or could spend their retirement years in life after they took the decision to retire and found them already retired, but not prepared or ill-prepared to spend their retirement years in the most enjoyable and productive way. People who are busy and productive workers are always in the habit of putting out one fire after another fire at their work places. Retirement will be the last thing they would entertain or worry about in their minds when they have to put out fires on a daily basis at work.

Retirement Planning:

All these years you worked for others, most probably for an employer who paid you for your time. You did not have time to think about yourself. Just like a carpenter who may not find time to build his own house, you worked harder and harder putting aside your own needs. This was because you were in the prime of your productive life, most probably supporting a family with children. As they grew older, you were more interested in their college education and future than your own life. You may have yearned to do many things in life, but there was no time or resources for you to do those things that you really wanted to do because you had to go to work to find the money to put bread and butter on your table to feed and educate your growing up children. Your yearning to do things in life got pushed to the back burner when other tasks and activities received priority.

The normal work routine of an average employee who does repeat business at work goes as follows: You go to work and you have an assigned office with all office equipment such as filing cabinets, telephones, computers etc., and a job description that tells you what to do to fill the time of the work day. To put it in another way, you will be spending the time available during the 8-hour work-day to complete the work assigned to you. Your job will be evaluated at the end of a week, a month or a year that keeps you or not in the job. Most working people's passion and the type of work they do at work do not necessarily go together. In the case of a small minority of all working people this may not be true. They may have really wanted to do the type of thing they do for a living at their work as well and therefore retirement would not add anymore benefit to their life's dreams than if they continued to work as previously in the same job and working environment.

Some type of work may also demand a person to be "married" to the job rather than having a life of her/his own. Most medical professionals and information technology workers may belong to this category due to the fact that they do provide essential services to people. It may be most possible that they have a reason to get up in the morning and go to work at 4:00 am even though they are expected to be at work at 8:00 a.m. Most often they do come home at 7:00 pm after work even though they are expected to leave work at 5:00 pm in the afternoon. They may even bring work home from their work place. Today, most work places have their own intranet and extranets that allow workers to do work more productively without limiting themselves to their specific work location/s. Consequently, besides the actual work that employees need to perform at work, they have additional training and learning needed to keep up with the rapidly changing technology that has become an essential part of almost every work that people do today.

Retirement time for spouses who worked all their life could be a challenge. This is about adjustment for a new way of life. Some people make the adjustment easily but other people find adjustment most difficult. Some CEO spouses would want to manage the house hold just the same way they did that in their companies after retirement. Some army navy or police officers would want to manage their households with the same rigorous rules regulations and schedules that they previously enforced at their work places. Such work routines die hard in people's life. This applies to both men and women who hold high ranking management and or commanding positions in large organizations. In worst case scenarios of conflict between retiree spouses, such couples may end up seeking psychiatric counsel since they cannot handle the situation by themselves.

One possible way to avoid conflict would be to plan a staggered retirement with the employer/s. This arrangement would enable working spouses to phase out of work gradually and at the same time allow them to gradually adjust to the new non-working flexible life style with no work stress in retired life at home. Nevertheless there are hard realities that every human being needs to face sooner or later in their life. Those who have the capacity to anticipate future events as they come to pass may most probably manage them gracefully. Retirement is one such decision that most working people have to think about and plan for sooner than later. Assuming that you have gotten to this place in life, you are old enough to retire from work, and you have unfulfilled passion in life that you always wanted to satisfy, you have your retirement project waiting for you to begin. All these years you worked for others. Now the time has come to you to work for yourself, even if it means not working at all!

How I planned my retirement – My personal life-long experience as a college professor

I had a 44-year-long career as an educator affiliated with universities in 3 different countries, 11 different universities and colleges, occupying 8 different positions in different universities and colleges ranging from lecturer to full-professor, three tenured faculty positions each of which lasted over 10 years in three different universities, and three sabbatical positions among many other moon-lighting and temporary type of occupations including consultation projects, that I held for shorter periods of time in industry as well.

Although changing positions this many times could be considered as a negative trait in the work world labeled as "job-hopping," it worked out to my advantage considering the amount of exposure I had in various different work environments and associations with professionals in my field of work. It also gave me the opportunity to be able to take risks in my career and at the same time to focus on my personal plans and goals, especially on developing thoughts on my plans to retire from the very early days of my employment life.

Early in my work life, I learned that most colleges and universities allow leave of absence either to take a break from doing the same type of routine work or to pursue additional learning on the job to catch up with the latest advancements in the field. These come as scholarships, fellowships, foreign job assignments, sabbatical leave of absence for short periods of time ranging from 6 months to 1 or two years. These are undoubtedly excellent opportunities that allow employees to take a break from the routine type of jobs that many of them do at most work places; sabbatical leave of absence ranging from one semester to one year granted to tenured faculty members who satisfy certain conditions and criteria in colleges and universities is one such valuable opportunity available to educators to refresh knowledge, publish articles in refereed journals or text books while allowing them to travel and work in different geographical locations sometimes in a foreign country at the same time.

I took my very first sabbatical leave of absence from university of Ceylon (currently Sri Lanka) in 1980 after serving 12 years in that university as a faculty member. Since I opted to take my leave as earned leave, the university kept my position for one year to return while at the same time I had one year to pursue my career options in other parts of the world without being overly attached to my original place of work.

Normally, most university faculty members are very concerned about their job security; they try very hard to keep the same job in which they gain tenure and get promoted from assistant to associate and full professor ranks over several years of service; some who are interested in university administrative type of work become heads of departments, deans, vice presidents and presidents of universities. Therefore, gaining stability, seniority and security in their positions after obtaining tenure in a university teaching position becomes very important to most university faculty members; a tenured faculty position serves not only as the first step in the door in a university career, but also a springboard to gain bigger and better positions of authority and power in their career ladder. The downside of such attachment to work places is that such workers find it very difficult to let go of their attachment to their work place even when it is time for them to do so. This is particularly true of faculty members who reach retirement age at colleges and universities. The same tendency of permanency of work is seen in the corporate world as well as in the other industries in which workers are very much concerned about the permanency of their jobs. Therefore, the opportunity available to obtain leave of absence granted by most work places to employees is one advantage they have, to spend at least one year in a different environment and away from the regular work places. This, in a way, is similar to a retreat in work and life during which a person has the freedom to reflect and re-think upon personal goals in life detached from work. My first sabbatical leave helped me to look at my work as it were, from a distance without being attached to my work place. It also gave me the freedom and insight needed to visualize and face my personal goals and expectations in life in a realistic way by switching my field of education as well as my career and career goals in life.

I took a second sabbatical leave of absence from Valley City State University of North Dakota in 1998 after having served that university for six years subsequent to obtaining tenure at that university. Sabbatical leave in most universities is considered earned leave for faculty members having tenure. Such leave can be obtained with half-pay, full-pay, or no-pay depending on the freedom and flexibility one wants to have to return to the same institution or not. I took my second sabbatical leave for one year on no-pay from Valley City State University in North Dakota with the assurance in writing that my position will be kept for me in that university for one year. It was again a delightful time in my life that I had time away from my routine and regular work, and had a salaried permanent position in another university in Mountain Home, Arkansas in which I had the opportunity of sharing my work experience with colleagues and students in a different geographical and educational environment. The most important part of this sabbatical leave of absence is that it gave me the insights needed to plan for my retirement more vigorously than before. Also during this year of absence, I had the opportunity to travel and see other parts of America, away from my regular place of work. I had one full year to compare my place of work in North Dakota with that of Arkansas and decide if I wanted to return to North Dakota or else to continue to work at the new place of work where I spent the sabbatical leave. At the end of the year, I decided to return to North Dakota since I wanted to keep residency there because my son wanted to go to medical school in North Dakota as a resident. I would have lost residency in North Dakota if I continued to stay in Arkansas and accepted a permanent position there. But, the planning time I had for my retirement and the material that I write in this book was mostly collected in my daily journals within that year that I had time to concentrate and research on retirement planning in addition to my work assignment as a professor in a two-year college in Mountain Home, Arkansas.

I took a third one-semester sabbatical leave of absence from Ferris State University in 2009 to spend one semester at University of Arkansas at Fayetteville, Arkansas, for doing a comparative study of the computing facilities, both software and hardware, available for teaching higher level computer information system courses in these two educational institutions. This was a leave of absence with pay from my place of work with a promise to return. The leave also gave me the flexibility to retire from Ferris State University at the end of the academic year 2011.

In reflecting upon my own work life, I consider myself very fortunate to have provided my service to three excellent educational institutions where I had tenure and leave of absence from work with perfect freedom and flexibility to plan for my future professional goals and retirement plans. Undoubtedly, separation from places of work and colleagues for good is a very traumatic experience most workers undergo as they tend to develop strong attachment to people and work places. I had far too many of such places that I had to leave behind, especially the first and the last universities. At the same time I am very grateful that I had the time away from these places of work, for which I was very much attached, and considered myself very much a part of. I have had the opportunity to witness a large number of workers, in almost every rank in those institutions, retiring at some point of their life either willingly or reluctantly or due to reasons such as poor health conditions beyond their control. Some of these ideas that I write come from my observations of real life experiences of real people.

The realization that we have to retire from work as much we love to work, naturally comes to every human being at some point in their life. In my case it came sooner than I thought mainly during my leave of absences from my regular work places. I had the marvelous opportunity to reflect upon my retirement plans during the three sabbaticals I had from three wonderful work places I served in my life. I am grateful for that. They helped me to plan my retirement and share my thoughts that I write in this book.

Insight # 3

There are three types of workers: 1) those who are strongly dependent on and attached to their work place, 2) those who have a tendency to overwork to the extent that they neglect their personal life, 3) those who are an asset to any work place they choose to work for and share their knowledge and experience as a service to that work place; they have the potential to grow together with any work place.

The third category of worker has less trouble in making their decision to retire from work at the proper time.

Chapter four

Retired, So What?

An end or a new beginning?

Due to advances of medical technology, most people in the world, especially in the west, currently enjoy longer life and are beginning to spend a longer time in retirement than they did before. Those who planned their retirement early in their life accumulate sufficient wealth that enables them to have a comfortable and financially stable life during the bonus years of retirement. The longer life they live and social security funds available to them during their retirement years are two benefits that most retirees of the baby boomers generation (those who were born between the years 1946 – 64 in the U.S.) enjoy today. Retirement is not just a man's dream anymore; most women work today, and they also retire either before, after, or together with their married spouses who retire from work. Like single retired men there are single retired women as well in today's retirement communities.

The purpose of this chapter is to highlight some of the activities most retirees do to fill the time of the day they have in their retirement years. After all they do not have to go for work anymore and they have all that time they used spend at work every day to devote to something else that they choose to do. However, many people give little thought as to how they would spend that free time in their retirement years ahead of them. This is a challenge that many retirees face at the beginning of their retirement – as to how they should spend the free time they have earned after retiring from work in order that they could fulfill their retirement dreams.

How most people spend their retirement life today:

So you are retired, and now what? Do you want to sleep most of your free time that you gained after retirement? Or else, do you want to watch TV all day long? These are probably the two most common activities that retired people engage in during their retirement years. Valuable information as to how people in the U.S. spend their time is available in Time Use Survey (ATUS) annual reports published in 2003-2013 (http://www.bls.gov/tus/). There are also other studies that analyze such data and statistics drawing conclusions based on these findings (http://www.bls.gov/opub/mlr/2007/05/art2full.pdf). As reported in ATUS surveys, an activity that most elderly people spend time besides sleeping, is watching TV. Accordingly, many old people watch 3.77 hours of TV daily.

There are many retirees who watch TV most of the day and late into the night. Their spouses make a pot of coffee; they drink coffee or beer, watch football, basketball, or baseball games, and cricket games in other parts of the world and cheer all day and night long. Some watch movies, and serials, talk about them with their friends, and wait to watch the next segment on the following day thinking about what is going to happen next. Most people today have HDTVs with large screens in the sitting rooms from where they could watch TV immediately and conveniently; it is also an inexpensive and passive source of entertainment and the natural tendency for most retirees is to spend a good part of their time of the day they used to spend at work, in front of a TV screen.

Children, Grand Children and Great Grand Children:

Strong family ties lead to a strong and cohesive family life. Such family members have family traditions passed down to family members for generations and members of those families are closely bonded and united. New births, birthday anniversaries, wedding and wedding anniversaries, marriages and marriage anniversaries and other occasions such as the memorial day, thanks giving, Christmas or other important days of other religions (if the family members are followers of other religions) are celebrated by the family members who get together for celebrating such occasions. Such closely-knitted family members have a tendency to live in close geographical proximity. The retired parents and grandparents of such families are adored by their grown up children, grand children, and in some instances by great grandchildren. Unfortunately, such strong and ideal families and close family relationships are currently on the decline. Most family members today have a tendency to live thousands of miles apart from one another due to work and other demands which preclude them from getting together even during family emergencies. As a consequence most growing up children of the current generation have a tendency to make their own independent decisions regarding even the most important matters in their life such as choosing their life-partners. Likewise, most elderly members of the families, especially males tend to spend a good part of their advanced years alone and in isolation.

There are other present-day retirees who grew up in families with strong family values, bonds, and attachment to their family members showing a tendency to be overly concerned about their own children as well as grandchildren to the extent that they spend most of their retirement years worrying about them. They keep thinking and talking about their kids, and grand kids never wanting to get off the subject. I have known many parents and grandparents who were very pre-occupied with the welfare of their own grown-up children as well as their grand children. The reader may have his or her close relatives who lived a lifetime of positive or negative relationships with their children as well as grandchildren. One old parent who was in my neighborhood once told me in a conversation he had with me that he learned the hard way, not to worry about his grown up kids when they reached the sexually active age. Many elderly family members, who go through difficult family relationships without even wanting to discuss it with others, even with their close friends or family, eventually take those problems with them to their graves.

On the contrary, some retirees can't wait to be with their grandkids. All that they want talk about is their grand kids. This may come perhaps as a guilt-trip of some grandparents who were so busy when their own children were young and they could not afford to give even five minutes of their time to their own growing up children due to their busy work schedules. The children of course would have had hundreds of hours with baby sitters and day-care centers, with television, growing up as latch-key kids. Most of the retirees will have their story to tell about their kids and their grandkids – those hobby horses that they do not want to get off.

As popular prime time television programs and radio talks would indicate, some retired parents and grandparents are even willing to participate in support groups when their children display bad behavioral problems. Others go for counseling sessions or undergo psychiatric therapy when they find their adolescent and adult children choose life styles that do not fit with their expectations. If the children are younger, some parents apparently send them to correctional facilities as the popular media have us believe.

Parenting and grand parenting episodes are dramatized in prime time sitcoms like "Everybody Loves Raymond." Conflicts between the old and the young people could have a very negative impact on the old people and could be avoided if such relationships that may cause difficulties are balanced and controlled, if not altogether avoided. One grandmother had tears in her eyes when she told me that the birthday-present she hauled across several states in mid-America was unappreciated and rejected by her son and her daughter-in-law. Another mother could not sleep during nights when she knew that her son would be jumping off an air plane in performing his duties as an air force officer. The reader may add to this list other worries that many other retired parents may have about their little boys and little girls have grown up to be adults and left home for good.

Some retired parents in the developing world who spend all their hard-earned money to send their kids abroad to study without realizing that they would most probably not come back home after they become professionally qualified to work in the developed part of the world, keep waiting till they come home someday. The only thing they want before they die is to see those children even for a few days. But unfortunately those children who are grown up and have seen better parts of the world with better living conditions and better economic and social standards have neither the time nor the freedom from their busy work schedules to visit home and spend time with their parents even if they really want to do it. With the prevalence of e-mail, the Internet and other web services like Facebook, Face time, Twitter, and Skype, some tech savvy parents and grandparents try to reach their children and grandchildren spending an enormous amount of time on distant communications. But, they hardly realize that retirement is a time that they have for themselves to enjoy their own life. Letting go is tough for some retirees, unless they take the time to figure out what they really want to achieve in their retirement years.

Empty Nest:

Most adults are susceptible to empty nest syndrome, which is a feeling of grief and loneliness they go through when their children leave home for the first time to attend college or live on their own. Adults who are dealing with stressful circumstances such as retirement are also very likely to experience this syndrome. This is one risk factor that retirees may want to take into consideration when they plan on their retirement. This is because symptoms of empty nest syndrome may lead to depression, a sense of loss of purpose, feelings of rejection, or worry, stress, and anxiety.

In order that they deal with this situation, some retirees spend enormous amount of time doing yard-work and house cleaning work after their retirement.

However, empty nesters do face new challenges, such as establishing a new kind of relationship with their children, having to find other ways to occupy their free time, reconnecting with each other, and finding ways to be happy when their children leave home. One of the easiest ways for adults to cope with empty nest syndrome is to keep in contact with their children. Technological developments such as cell phones, text messaging, and the internet all allow for increased communication between parents and their children these days unlike in the past. Retired parents going through empty nest syndrome can ease their stress and sadness by pursuing their own hobbies and interests in their increased spare time. Networking with relatives, friends, families, or professionals may help them. Thus empty nester adults can rekindle their own relationship by spending more time together.

There can be many unproductive things that retirees do aimlessly during their retirement years. For instance, there was a retiree who kept watching the trains that go by his house that faced the highline bridge of Valley City, North Dakota, all day long. He did this daily routine until the day he died. It was a sad story of an old man who was lonely and had nothing else to do in his retirement days. He did not plan for his retirement and he spent his retirement years watching the trains go by his house. His grown up son who told me this story could not help his father to stop his train-watching behavior. His mother who was a retired school teacher was unable to help her husband either. The reader may be able to relate this incident to her/his experiences with retired people who were lonely and depressed without being able to connect themselves to the world that they belonged to earlier in their life.

In this respect, a proper understanding of how retired people use their time is important because it affects their well-being. Although Psychological and sociological research indicates the importance of being socially engaged throughout the aging process of people, very little attention has been paid to study and analyze as to how retired people spend their non-working free time is positively or negatively affecting their life. Such an understanding is important not only to family members of retiring or retired people, but to those people themselves who plan to lead a happy life in their retirement.

A Personal Note:

In my case, I always wanted to do my own writing. I was not at all interested if people cared to read what I write or not. But I know that there will be someone somewhere who would read it, appreciate it and learn some things from what I had to say in my writings. So long as I get those thoughts across that kept popping up in my head in a sensible and readable way I am satisfied.

Writing gives me a sense of fulfillment. Journal writing was something that I started doing a long time ago. It became a habit so much so that I had a bundle of journals that I always carried with me and wanted to revise and re-write as a compendium of memoirs. As computers became popular, I started writing my journals electronically. It was at times confusing because of the rapid changes in computer hardware and software. Keeping track of those writings done on so many different word processors using different computer hardware and operating systems was a challenge. My writings were on six-inch floppies, 3 ½ inch floppies, zip disks, and flash drives until recently. Now with free virtual space provided by many companies promoting web logs (blogs), I have started posting my writings online. Facebook is another platform on which I post my writings in other languages as well that I am familiar with. Even this piece of writing that I do now has been in my mind for a long time collected in the form of daily journals. I consider collecting my thoughts on retirement that I had been writing down in the form of memoirs just as I entered my retirement phase of life as a much better alternative than sitting in front of the TV and sipping coffee or beer all day long. Most importantly, the writing that I do gives me great satisfaction, enjoyment and a sense of self-actualization. It gives me a most liberating experience. But I do not necessarily want to recommend my way of spending my retirement to others; this is because I respect the things that others may have in mind to do that they are passionate about. It is up to them to find what makes them happy rather than what others would tell them to do in their retirement. Many of us have untapped potential within us that have never been explored and waiting to be explored by ourselves. The key to opening such potential is within us.

Some Concluding Thoughts:

As mentioned earlier, if 100 retirees were asked the question as to what they would like to do in their retirement phase of life, you would undoubtedly get many different answers. You won't be surprised if such a thought may not have even occurred to some of people. I have had the chance of observing many retirees who were not only a burden to others but a burden to themselves as well. This was not because they became incapable of taking care of them, but because they got into a state of depression from which they did not have the capability of snapping out. The state of mind they were in gradually declined and undermined the control they had over their own life. Such deterioration of the state of mind naturally leads to physical deterioration resulting in unhappiness and hopelessness. They get depressed and consequently they will have family disputes, they lose control of their life and feel unwanted and neglected by their loved ones. All the money that such people saved for retirement may not be as much help as the happiness, contentment and hope of life they very much need at this time of their life. These are people who allow others, including their loved ones to feel that they are useless and unwanted. There is therefore a very good reason for the retirees not to allow others, including their loved ones, to control their thoughts and life. Those retirees who are in charge of their own life, not only are able to help themselves but also others who are around them.

The bottom line is finding out as to what you really want to do in your life within the retirement years of your life. You need to satisfy that desire/s in such a way that it will make you and your loved ones happy. Your loved ones should understand and appreciate your desire to accomplish what you always wanted to do. You need to feel that you are appreciated valued and respected for who you are, what you are, what you want, and what you do. This may not be just one thing; but a variety of things that you always wanted to do like traveling, fishing, cooking gardening or bird watching, meditating, yoga etc. Unless you know what you always wanted to do or else explored and found out at least during this stage of your life, and make it obvious to your loved ones as to what makes you happy in your retirement life, there is the possibility that others will tell you what you need to do for them, unfortunately. You won't like to be in that plight when others would dictate to you what you should be doing. You are retired, you do not work for others and you want to have the best time of your life doing what you really wanted to do in your life, and at the same time making others who love you to be happy.

Insight # 4
Time wastes us. There is a good reason for retirees to conserve the time they have for themselves rather than wasting it.

If we live 100 years, we will be spending 100 x 365 x 24 x 60 = 52,560,000 minutes which is the entire life time that is available to us. If we spend ¼ of our lifetime in retirement we will be spending 13,140,000 minutes in retirement. But unfortunately, most of us have a tendency not to think about such realities of life, unless they are faced with a life threatening and a terminal illness from which they suffer. Although technology has enabled human beings to do work faster and made the world smaller, it has significantly shortened the time humans have for themselves by enabling them to do multitasking that virtually robs the real time that humans have for themselves. There is therefore a good reason for us to use technology to work for us rather than against us, especially during our retirement phase of life.

Chapter Five

A Place To Retire

Home is where you say it is

This chapter discusses some of the planning you need to do well ahead of your retirement in order that you find the best location to live in your retirement years. Such planning takes time and information gathering. Someone else's retirement plan may not suit you because you are your own person. You need to plan your retirement in such a way that it helps you to live happily during the years you have ahead of you. If you have a partner with whom you could plan your retirement together, it is best that you and your partner plan your retirement location together in such a manner that the location that you both choose to retire will make both of you happy. You and your partner may most probably not agree on all the detailed criteria relating to your ideal retirement location, but it is important that you plan it together than by one person only. After all, most married partners may have lived a long period of their life together facing many challenges in life that include raising and educating their children, if they had any, that they brought together into this world. Therefore, why not plan your retirement as well together to suit the expectations of both partners than only one partner? The focus of this chapter is however, not necessarily the retirees who are married. The ideas discussed may apply to single, widowed or others who are unmarried and living with others, who are planning a retirement home together.

Some considerations for retirement location planning may include and not limited to are: 1) staying where you are with no intention to move at all, 2) moving into a retirement community, 3) moving to a location where you could buy or build your own dream home for retirement, 4) having a lake home or retirement home where you could spend summer in one location, winter in another location, weekends in a lake house etc. in addition to the regular permanent home where you normally live during a good part of the year, depending on the availability of resources a retiree could afford to spend on her/his retirement life. There may be other such variations of living arrangements during retirement that the reader may consider depending on her/his desires and plans. The pluses and minuses of each of these plans need to be weighed before one makes a final decision in the planning stage. For instance, if one wants to move into a retirement community exclusively to spend one's retirement, one has to investigate and do research up front on several such retirement communities regarding the expenses involved, facilities available, and other restrictions, and management styles of those retirement community properties. Some retirement communities are gated and may incur additional costs for some services that you may not even want to use, that are not always desirable as far as you are concerned. The property owners' association dues generally referred to as "commons" in such places could be something that you may not have any control over, and property managers could be changing in some retirement communities in quick succession; they may change rules and regulations as well as the property owners' association dues as they take over the management in such communities. It is therefore prudent to investigate any retirement community that you are interested in to move into by getting all the information ideally by visiting those places that you have narrowed down and spending at least a few days there or gathering information on them by doing online searches and making your own observations and judgments about such communities before you make a commitment to move into such places and find that you made a mistake in choosing to live in that place.

Moving to a new location:

Location, location, location is a key success factor in real estate business. Any successful real estate broker or sales person will tell you about the importance of the wisdom in living in the best location. But what is the best location that may suit a retiree? Is it on a top of a mountain from where they could see the rest of the people living down below? Or is it just near the airport from where they could take off and land as they please? Or else, is it just by the hospital so that they could quickly visit the hospital when they are sick? Or is it near the shopping center where they could do shopping conveniently? The reader may add all other ideal locations of her/his choice to this list. The reality however is that the best location to live during ones retirement could not be the same for every retiree; it may also not be the same place for the same retiree as s/he lives though different phases of her/his retirement years either.

Some consideration for selecting the location of one's retirement home by a retiree could be as follows. This assumes that s/he has the capability and resources as well as the desire to make such a choice. A decision table with all the criteria (both positive and negative) may enable a retiree to make a sound decision of the ideal place that s/he wants to retire and enjoy life during the last phase of life. It is most important that one tries out at least a few of these ideal places by living in those locations at least for a short period of time by taking a vacation in such selected spots in order that s/he validates the choice with reality.

Weather and environmental issues:

We all love good weather with temperature ranging from 65 - 70 degrees Fahrenheit. Some of us have had experience living in below zero degree weather, snow during 5 months of the year, hurricanes, tornadoes, floods and other bad weather conditions during our life time when we did not have the choice of moving out of such areas because we had a good job that paid us well albeit the weather was inclement. However we all love the greenery, scenery, mountains, parks, rivers, sea shores etc. Some people who retire may have sacrificed living and enjoying in those prime locations during the prime of their life because they may not have had the choice of moving into areas where the weather and the natural environment was great. They may have hesitated to take risks as far as their careers were concerned, and were happy in such comfort zones as far as their work was concerned, and were willing to live through bad weather conditions in those locations where they had their desired jobs, careers, and professions. Some retirees may have not only had their secure jobs, but the schools that their children used to love and the junior-high and high-school kids in those locations their children made friends with etc. But retirement could be a time they are possibly free to find the best location that they like most to live. The only limitation that they may possibly have is the amount of time that they have to enjoy the best years of their life. There is a good reason therefore for potential retirees to select the dream location where they always wanted to live. It may or may not perhaps be where they currently live.

Economy and cost of living issues:

Cost of living in the area where we want to retire is a consideration for most of us when we have to live on a fixed income and a fixed budget during our retirement. This is because we need to spend the money in the best possible way so that we could get the best value of money when we live on a fixed income during our retirement years. For instance, the cost of living in certain areas in the world could be so prohibitive to live in those areas unless you have an unlimited source of money to spend during your retirement years. As an example, I would prefer a state that has no property taxes and/or minimum sales tax over a state that has high state income and property as well as probate taxes. Selecting a state (country or island) that has marginal or no income tax could save you a considerable amount of money to spend on other necessities of life during your retirement years.

The cost of living in all locations in the world is not the same. It is very economical to live in areas that are not densely populated. House price in some states of the United States for instance, could be so prohibitive to live in those states. As an example, a house that just fits the lot with no yard at all in Hawaii could cost a few million dollars whereas a similar house built on a half an acre of land lot would not even cost one fourth of that price in some states like Arkansas where the weather is great. The logic is clear. It is prudent that the future retirees should invest some time researching on the cost of living-condition factors in the areas that would attract her/him most before making a decision to move into that location and find things short of expectations after the move and be very unhappy about the decision made to move there. This is true of medical expenses as well. In some states of the United States, it costs more in medical expenses than in others. With the accessibility of the Internet and the availability of excellent search engines like Google, one could do information gathering with ease provided one has the interest and passion to do so. After all who would buy a car today without checking the prices and performance factors using the Internet or the latest issue/s of Consumer Reports magazine? Wouldn't spending time on such a venture for at least a couple of years before one retires be a most productive way of planning for a happy retirement in a location s/he would be happy?

Family, acquaintances and friends:

Some retirees would be very much interested in living closer to their sons and daughters, relatives, acquaintances, and friends during their retirement years whereas other retirees would not want to live close to them at all. Depending on their family structures, family values, relationship patterns, and individual preferences, some retirees would want to live in areas that are not too close or not too far away from their close family, acquaintances, relatives and friends. As we all know, family life has evolved within the last few centuries from extended to single family taking many different turns including the addition of same-sex marriages as another form of marriage and family life. Many families and retirees would be struggling with such issues within their own families wanting to find the best way they could live their retired life and let their loved ones live their life in the best possible way that suits them. The best thing under such circumstances is to live in a location where one would not make others problems her or his problem and at the same time live in a place where there is the least amount of family related mental worries during the retirement years. The same mode of retirement life style will not fit all retirees; the best possible suggestion is that each future retiree takes time to determine if s/he wants to relocate after retirement, and if so, as to what would be the best possible dream location s/he would spend the retirement years that fits her criteria best before she makes the decision to do so. After all if one is not willing even to make an attempt to try and see how a move could impact the quality of one's retirement life, one is completely depriving oneself of that golden opportunity that is just waiting for the taking.

Recreation:

Recreation is most essential during retirement. Retirement stage of your life is the time that you need to spend a good part of your day every day for recreation purpose. It goes without saying that retirement is not the best time to spend most of your day time vegetating in front of a TV or surfing the net or aimlessly spending enormous amount of time on social networks that are popping up on the web these days. Recreation could be biking, fishing, walking, golfing or jogging with real friends or engaging in any other such activities that the reader may include in her/his list. The interest of every individual retiree may be somewhat different. Some would like to read books as recreation and some would like to listen to music or play musical instruments while others would like to sit under a tree doing nothing at all. It may not be just one thing but a variety of things that one may want to do while enjoying the day. Nevertheless, a retiree could not afford to skip recreational activities that include, walking and or other forms of physical activities that will be essential to maintain a healthy body and healthy mind.

Getting your retirement home constructed:

Getting a dream house constructed before you retire could also be one of the options some retirees may have. Most locations of your choice are likely to have builders who will be able to help you build the house of your dreams within a reasonable amount of time.

There are advantages and disadvantages to getting a house constructed over buying one. It all depends on whether you are going to settle for a house that has already been constructed to satisfy the demands of most consumers or you have your own specific requirements that will only be satisfied by a custom built house. This is because there is no guarantee that a house you buy would make you absolutely happy satisfying all your requirements and expectations. For instance, if you want a house with a built-in tornado shelter or handicap accessible bathroom and/or master bedroom on the ground floor, you may have a very limited choice or zero choice in finding such a house in the geographical area that attracts you most. The only choice you may have in such a situation would be to find a buildable lot and a builder to build your dream house to satisfy all your specific needs. This is one more reason that you should plan to find your retirement home well ahead of your retirement. You need at least a few years to do the research needed to find the location that attracts you most, create a suitable model of your dream house, and find a suitable builder, designer, and financial plan. For instance, you may need to decide if you want to handle the construction loan yourself or allow the construction company that you select to build your house and handle all financial matters as well. If this is the first time you get a house constructed in your life, you may have to spend a considerable amount of time with friends or acquaintances who have got a house constructed before and have had the experience of doing such an activity so that you may perhaps avoid possible pitfalls associated with the process. This is because you want the best and nothing but the best when you are prepared to spend the time, energy and your hard-earned money to get your dream house constructed instead of buying a house that is available for sale by someone who had lived there and owned it, and is willing to sell it to you.

There are many other considerations that need careful thinking through and planning before building your house. Most of such considerations apply to search of houses available for resale as well. Some of these considerations could be: lot size, floor area, number of bed-rooms and bath rooms, whether one floor or two floors, basements, number of garages (one, two or three), elevation of the driveway to the house from the road, which direction the house is facing (a house facing the east would have lots of sunshine most of the day and snow would melt quickly during winter), dimensions of the master bed room and other bedrooms, and the neighborhood where the house is located. The reader may have many other features on her/his wish list such as a swimming pool, formal dining room, patio, cooking and grilling facilities in a shaded area detached from the main house etc.

Most importantly, a retiree needs to recognize that maintenance of large houses with a large yard could not only be difficult but also expensive and unnecessary. This is your retirement home, and most retirees are on a fixed income. Maintaining a large house that includes a large tax bills (federal, state and city taxes), high insurance premiums, water, electricity bills, and lawn maintenance depending on the location of the house, could add up quickly. For example, if two people were to live in a house all year round, with the possibility of children visiting them for a few days within the year, it will be very unwise to maintain a house with 4-5 bedrooms, cleaning, heating and cooling them all year round. The larger the floor area of a house is, the more expensive it is to maintain it. The chances are that you may not be able to do the house cleaning yourself as you did when you were young. You will most probably be spending a few hundred dollars weekly to get your house cleaned. These expenses will be discussed in detail in the next chapter.

One advantage you have in building your retirement house instead of buying one that had already been constructed, is that you have the option to construct your dream house that fits your house maintenance budget within your means. In the case of buying your dream house, the drawback is that you will fall in love with a resale-house that you like most, but you will most probably not like the maintenance bills as you continue to live in it.

Insight #5

The location of your dream home where you plan to spend your retirement years undoubtedly plays a major role in how you feel, both physically and mentally. The longer you put off planning your retirement home, the shorter time you are going to enjoy living in it. It takes a considerable amount of time to make the house that you buy or build, your own "home." This is because homes cannot be bought or built in a few days. The longer you live in a place, the more it becomes your home and more it is precious to you as your residence. You will be a happy retiree in your heart if you have a home that you love to come home to, and wake up peacefully every morning in your home being able to connect yourself to the natural beauty of the environment and neighborhood in which it is built. There is no place like your own dream home.

Chapter Six

Budget Your Retirement

Money matters, but a budget matters more

We all need money to live. The reality about money is that we cannot spend it if we do not have it. But with the wide spread popularity of credit cards, most people often spend money that they do not have and get into debt in a hurry and stay in debt for a good part of their lifetime without knowing about it and without doing anything about it either, only making minimum payments thereby going into debt deeper and deeper as the interest on credit cards gets compounded. Same goes for home mortgages and car liens if taken without doing the necessary mathematical calculations necessary for repayment plans in detail. This is where a good budget matters most to us to spend our money prudently.

During the time you have a stable income and high-salaried employment, any bank would reach out to lend you money. This is because you are considered a credit worthy person by the banks. Think about the mortgage you are expected to pay for your house over 30 years. You pay approximately three times the worth of the house to settle your debt (if at all you paid the very last mortgage payment). If you plan your income and expenses of your household well with a sound budget, you could be paying down your mortgage sooner, perhaps in 15 years instead of 30 years by making additional principal payment on your house mortgage payment and saving all that money that you would have otherwise paid as mortgage interest.

Presuming you worked for others or was self-employed all your life time, you may have not had time to think about your own life other than your work and how to perform better and more efficiently at your work place. Those who devoted their entire productive life, especially those "child-centered" parents, "house-proud" and/or "eating out" and "vacation happy" folks, may not have had any time to plan for their retirement years except continuing the same type of repeat business at work. For many people, it is all about the work- place, their children, houses, automobiles and nothing else.

It is assumed in this chapter that retirees who leave their work would have saved a substantial amount of money, possess a house that they fully own and have other assets and no liabilities such as outstanding automobile loans, house mortgages, or worse, credit card debts. It is also assumed that they do not belong to the poverty line.

This chapter discusses some essential considerations that retirees may have to make as they enter their retirement phase of life no matter what location they choose to live in (Chapter 5) or life style they may want to adopt for living - married, single, divorced, widowed, living with significant others etc. Those who begin their retirement phase of life with the end in mind having figured out a plan that fits them, will certainly save a lot of grief in the long run as far as money is concerned as they enter the retirement phase of life.

The best time to do retirement planning:

If a retiree has not taken the time to do retirement planning, the best time to do so is before it is too late. One best method of quickly learning the tricks of the trade is to attend seminars given by reputable companies for free. As it happens, information about most people, in particular their age, is available to business enterprises however much they promise to protect our privacy.

You may most probably be contacted by phone, e-mails, and/or regular mail about the retirement planning seminars in your area several times within the year as you approach retirement age. It would be best that a prospective retiree attends at least three such seminars, listen with intent to learn and study the handouts and workbooks given in these seminars. Most of these seminars run for a few hours. The topics covered are mostly, tax reduction plans, reducing tax on social security, estate planning, long term healthcare concerns, pros and cons of wills and trusts etc. Although the intent of offering these free seminars is to enroll retiree clients who would seek accounting, legal and financial as well as tax advice for a fee, the information one could gather in these seminars for free would be extremely valuable in drawing up an affordable retirement plan that fits your needs. It is a part of the learning process of planning your retirement life. Most importantly the information that one gathers will enable at least some retirees to prevent probate on their accumulated wealth including real estate that they owned before they die. Although a revocable trust properly drawn by an attorney would cost somewhere around $ 2000 – 4000, it would be a very small amount to pay when compared to the legal hassle that entails if one were to die without such a plan. After all, it will be too late to try to prevent probate when a retiree with substantial amount of accumulated wealth has already died without a plan that would prevent probate on the assets that s/he possessed.

Just as an example of how a revocable trust works, consider the case of a husband and wife who employ legal counsel to draw up a revocable trust during their retirement phase of life. The husband and wife will be the joint trustees of the revocable trust. If one of them becomes incapacitated or dies, the survivor becomes the trustee with no probate lawyers or judges involved. When the survivor becomes incapacitated or dies the successor trustee/s (beneficirie/s) become the heirs of the trust. The distribution of the assets will be done according to the conditions stipulated in the trust and no probate lawyers or judges will be involved in the distribution of the wealth and real estate involved. The readers are advised to seek legal counsel on the information provided here from reputable attorneys who draw up such revocable trusts for a fee.

Importance of budgeting your expenses:

Your most important challenge before you enter your retirement years is to budget your spending in such a way that the assets that you own do not completely exhaust before you die. But no one has the capacity or wisdom to foresee when exactly (year, date, and time) s/he is going to die. The challenge is to make the money available to work for you until the end of your life, taking future inflation into consideration. Faced with this situation, it is best that you spend some time regularly studying about the best way to manage your money. Retirees who do not have such knowledge or experience may find it extremely rewarding and a beneficial thing to do in their retirement years. Such an involvement would not only help them to keep their minds alert and occupied, but also understand how to manage their hard-earned money as they desire. They will also be able to ask sensible questions from the financial advisers. The best time to study, learn and plan your money is the time when your brains are still alert and active. It makes sense to do such planning well before the time when you are unable to do so.

As mentioned earlier, most books written on retirement are mainly focused on money management. But how much money do you want? How much money could you or should you spend during your retirement years to lead a comfortable life? As we all know there is no limit to the greed humans do have. One book on retirement that I read mentioned a retiree who had accumulated $7 million. Yet he was unable to sleep peacefully at night because he was worried that the $7 million would not be enough for him to live on until he dies. This is not an unusual story. Therefore some retirees tend to spend a good part of their energy on making more and more money during retirement.

Faced with budgeting of financial needs during retirement period of life, a retiree may want to ask the following questions to budget her/his financial needs on a monthly basis. Given below is such a list:

1. Expenses on taxes, insurance, upkeep, maintenance, and utility bills (assuming that all mortgages are paid up).
2. Expenses on food, transportation, clothes, entertainment including telephone and computers (assuming that there are no outstanding lien on vehicle/s, and expenses on maintaining them are accounted for in the retirement budget).
3. Expenses involving travel, assuming that a retiree wants to travel places vacationing during her/his retirement.
4. Expenses involving medical insurance, long-term care insurance, annual medical checkups, doctor visits, and medications etc.
5. A debt reduction/ elimination plan if a retiree has outstanding debts (it is assumed that this would not be necessary if a retiree does not have outsanding debts to deal with).
6. Other miscellaneous expenses.
7. Emergency expenses.
8. A saving plan for unspent money within a given month.
9. The final expenses (funeral expenses).

Assuming that each person's requirements are different, it will be a very helpful exercise to prepare an individual budget that gives the total amount of monthly expenditure needed in one's retirement years by each and every retiring person. Such a budget will give the necessary insights as well as peace of mind that one very much needs during her/his retirement years. It is important that a retiree identifies those expenses upfront and prepare her/his monthly budget and learns to live a comfortable life within that budget. As you see already, the process and management of your retirement years involves spending time on yourself. You may have not have been able to do this before when you had to give all your time to others to make a living during all your working life.

A sample budget (income and spending plan) of a middle-class two retirees is given below:

Assumptions:

Two retirees are living in one house.

House is paid up and no outstanding mortgages are due on the house.

Three bedroom and two bath room house with approximately 3000 square feet floor area.

The house is situated in a location that has neither too low nor too high real estate taxes.

Two automobiles are used in the household.

Category	Description	Monthly	Annual
Housing	Real estate taxes	$500	$6000
	Home Insurance	$125	$1500
	Utility bills (water, electricity and gas + garbage collection)	$300	$3600
	Phone, cell-phones and Internet connections	$200	$2400
	Home Insurance	120	1440
Automobile/s (2)	Auto-insurance	$200	$2400
	Gas	$300	$3600
	License	$20	$240
	Maintenance	$200	$2400
Food	Groceries	$400	$4800
Pets	Food	$10	$120
	Veterinarian	$50	$600
	Pet care (when traveling)	$50	$600
Personal	Healthcare Insurance	$750	$9000
	Long-term care	$350	$4200
	Clothing	$100	$1200

Entertainment	Travel	$500	$6000
	TV	$60	$720
Miscellaneous		$500	$6000
Total		**$ 4735**	**$56,820**

In order to generate $56,820.00 for spending, one needs to allow at least an additional 25% of tax on the total budgeted expenses due as federal, state, and city taxes which are approximately another $14,205. Taking such tax commitments into consideration, the annual expenses of two retirees would be 56,820.00 + 14, 205.00 (federal and state and city taxes) = 71,025.00 computed at the rate of year 2014 calculations. These numbers have not taken inflation into consideration. The normal inflation rate is 4% every year and this means the buying power of every dollar will be 4% less every year as they progress. There is no guarantee that health-care and long-term care expenses will remain the same either.

A possible income plan for retirement spending:

Assumptions:

Both retiree/s have social security income
The retiree/s have required minimum distributions income coming from retirement funds accumulated from contributions made by the employee as well as the employer during at least a 25 years of work-life. (This fund is estimated to be one million dollars)
Other assets invested in growth funds
No liabilities other than the taxes they need to pay on the income from tax deferred annuities IRAs and other such savings.

An income plan for generating the funds needed for budgeting a retirement plan is therefore critical if one wants to avoid unnecessary financial worries during her/his retirement years. The following income plan gives an idea as to how a retiree should be funding her/his above spending plan taking into consideration 4% inflation for each year that s/he expects to live in retirement.

If you are 62 – 66 years old and worked most of your life in America you will be collecting social security income that will be calculated according to a formula taking each person's work history into consideration by the social security administration. If a person wants to know how much s/he will receive as social security benefits, she can find it online by going to the website www.ssa.gov.

Social security benefits in America started during President Franklin Roosevelt's time in 1935 and cost of living adjustments (COLA) for these benefits were started in 1975. Most workers today worry about the continuity of social security benefits for future workers; nevertheless the retirees of today should consider themselves most fortunate to be able to reap the benefits of their contributions that they made to social security administration in their retirement years.

Social Security in the United States is funded through payroll taxes called Federal Insurance Contributions Act Tax (FICA) and/or Self Employed Contributions Act Tax (SECA). Tax deposits are collected by the Internal Revenue Service (IRS) and are formally entrusted to the Federal Old-Age and Survivors Insurance Trust Fund, the Federal Disability Insurance Trust Fund, the Federal Hospital Insurance Trust Fund, or the Federal Supplementary Medical Insurance Trust Fund which comprise the Social Security Trust Funds. With a few exceptions all salaried income has a FICA and/or SECA tax collected on it.... Nearly all working (and many non-working) residents since Social Security's 1935 inception have had a Social Security number since it is required to do a wide range of things from paying the IRS to getting a job(source: http://en.wikipedia.org/wiki/Social_Security_(United_States)).

Social Security earnings approximately $40,000.00

Pensions 00

Retirement funds managed by professional wealth management firms =
$ 1,000000

Funds in IRAs and ROTH IRAS $50,000

Interest earning investments in emergency funds $100,000

	Monthly	Annual
Social Security Benefits	$3333.00	$40,000.00 (85% of SS earnings are taxable, only 34,000 will be available as income)
Monthly income from Retirement savings funds	$3000.00	$36,000.00
Federal and State Taxes to be paid (from tax table of 2013-jointly filing)	$(801.00)	$ (9611.00)
State tax varies depending on the state, may vary	(325) For 50,000 and over the tax in some states like Arkansas is $2570 + 7% of the excess over $ 49,999	$(3970.00)
Total Monthly income	$4701.58	$56419.00
Deficit	(33.41)	(401)

As we see in the above hypothetical example, our income is not sufficient to meet all our expenses when we take the federal and state tax liabilities as well as inflation into consideration. This certainly demonstrates the usefulness of a budget. The most important reason for retirees to do her/his budget is that it gives them a clear insight as to how they could adjust the budget in order that they live within that budget. In the above budget for example, a retiree may not spend as much as $6000 for travelling every year. The unused funds could be rolled over to subsequent years or into a savings account. If they decide to manage with one automobile instead of two as accounted for, there will be an additional annual saving of approximately $4,000 which may be used for either saving or any other needed expense. Budgeting is undoubtedly a powerful tool in the hands of anybody who wants to get the most out of the available funds.

Conclusions:

Many countries in the world have some sort of social security programs for older citizens. However, the details of how such funds are computed and administered are not similar. Some countries do have pension schemes only for the government servants for life. Some employers have provident funds for their employees in place of pensions. Some governments give free money as handouts to older people who are unable to work.

In addition to social security funds, most workers in America have the opportunity to contribute to tax deferred annuities through their work-life, a certain allowable contribution every year. There are other such tax-deferred saving methods like contributing to IRAs and Roth IRAs for qualifying workers. These saving methods allow workers to withhold payment of federal and state taxes until they are over 55 or retired, enabling them to pay reduced taxes at the time when they are retired and earning less income from cashing out their retirement funds. Many other countries have similar saving methods that help people in their retirement. In our example, the two retirees had most of the money they needed in their retirement coming from their social security benefits and annuities. The annuities are distributed over a specified period of time or over life-time depending on the wishes of a retiree. While a certain percentage is distributed on a progressively increased percentage level in keeping with the age of the retiree, the remainder of the funds is invested and therefore the chances are that such annuitized funds would guarantee cash flow every successive year of a retiree with a reduced balance remaining over the life time of a retiree, if such a decision was made beforehand.

In most Asian countries, people tend to make investment in real estate or other valuable properties and not necessarily in retirement funds. Some of them make investment in lucrative commercial properties. However, the downside of making such investments is that the money invested in such assets is not liquid, and one has to wait, sometimes indefinitely to cash out the proceeds of such investments. Retirement time of a person would not perhaps be the best time for such risky financial activities.

All in all, the more liquid all available funds are, the better they could be managed during a retirees life time. Some people reverse mortgage their houses when they do not have anyone to pass on their assets to, after their death. This is something that needs to be carefully considered before making a commitment, especially because such decisions and commitments could be irreversible.

Insight # 6

A sound financial plan that details all your assets and liabilities will give you a worry free retirement life.

Drawing up a budget based on your income and expenses based on your personal finances is therefore of utmost impotance. Doing such a plan yourself by learning the tricks of the trade will provide you with a road map for a happy retirement. Even if you break even during your years of retirement, you will still have enough equity in your assets to pass on to your children or loved ones or for charitable purposes if you learn how to manage money sensibly. A sound budget that pays, will certainly do this trick.

Chapter Seven

Health Is Wealth

Wealth is no guarantee for health

Wealth is measured in terms of our external material possessions. Our health on the other hand, is something that we really own and carry with us within ourselves at all times. Health can be measured, but not by the same criteria that we measure our wealth. We may be able to fix our health problems by consulting very expensive medical professionals and by undergoing very expensive major medical procedures and using very expensive medications life-long. Today people do heart transplantations, hip replacements, knee replacements and all sorts of body-part replacements, transplantations as well as plastic surgeries depending on their ability to pay the medical bills in terms hundreds of thousands of dollars. While life expectancy is on the rise due to improved medical innovations and services on the one hand, only a small fraction of retirees may perhaps be truly enjoying the happiness of being perfectly healthy and free from major medical problems on the other. Life prolonged by life support systems does not necessarily guarantee quality of life, peace of mind, and happiness. In this respect healthy people who do not have millions of dollars accumulated in wealth management finance companies, could be truly wealthier than the rich people in poor health.

As most of us know, the health problems most retirees suffer from may not necessarily be genetically caused. The life-style of the young and restless years of most people's life contributes to their health problems in their old age than most other factors. Common mistakes done by people who repent for having done them when they were in their 'young and restless years', may include consuming unhealthy food, excessive drinking of alcohol, smoking, using narcotic drugs, and excessive abuse of their body. It is very unfortunate that a true understanding of the causal relationship of bad behavior and health/medical problems that show up in their body come to most people in their last stages of life or in their death bed.

When I was a kid one of my uncles told me that there are three enemies to human beings. They are: 1) the devil 2) the other people in the world, and 3) oneself. I thought it was a profound thought of someone who had lived a full life who could share with others his wisdom before he departed this world. Also, I thought the saying brings home the fact that more than the devil or other people, a person her/himself could be the real enemy of her/himself. My uncle who told me this story was a very heavy drinker. His only happiness in life was drinking alcohol. He developed liver complications early in his life, endured untold suffering, and was miserable in the hospital for several months before he passed away in a state of coma. How unfortunate it was, I thought, for a person who handed me such words of wisdom, did not truly understand what he told me when I was a kid. Either he was not serious about what he said at the time he shared his wisdom with me, or he jolly well knew what ailed him and was killing him from within himself, but was unable to control his addiction to alcohol, similar to a moth that gets attracted to fire and eventually get burned by the fire. Some people are like that; they are in denial of what they do suffer from and do not want to correct them or admit it either.

Work and Health:

Apart from the above mentioned causes for ill-health that most people go through in their golden age, another most insidious-cause related to ill-health can be, work. People do all sorts of work during most of their productive life. Some do blue-collar work and some do white collar-jobs, some are engaged in 'professional work' with very high sounding titles attached to their name, like CEO or CIO of such and such a company etc. Most people have a life-long dream and passion to be associated with big companies in which the employees wear tie and suit every day to work and earn a handsome salary.

Employers would like to have their employees who work smarter than harder and want to hire and retain employees at all levels who are willing to put extra hours of work even during the weekends. I tend to worry about contract workers who do highway construction work breathing dust 8 hours a day, some doing heavy duty road digging with hand held heavy-duty equipment. A semi driver once told me that most number of years they could drive those big vehicles without having to face major health problems is 10 years. The executive jobs could be no better since their jobs entail tremendous mental stress. Certain jobs, especially in the private sector and in corporations have a high level of stress. In several studies of various populations over the years, scientists have found that deaths from heart attacks follow a pattern during the week. They occur at their lowest rates on weekends, jump significantly on Mondays, and then drop again on Tuesdays (Source: http://www.nytimes.com/2006/03/14/health/14real.html?_r=0).

It is common knowledge among most workers that Friday is a day for pink slips. Job performance is evaluated in shorter cycles in companies today with the advancement of technology. Having been associated closely with workers unions in several states, the author had the opportunity of listening to the grievances of a large number of workers across several states of America. They fit into a common pattern of complaints by workers against their supervisors' unreasonable expectations. Unfortunately, most workers faced with ill-treatment at work are willing to leave their jobs because they are fearful about their careers and future job prospects as well as negative publicity about them in their future work places. They therefore choose to voluntarily leave their jobs.

Working under such circumstances described above, few workers realize the importance of keeping the balance between their personal life and work life. As a result there is a tendency for their life to become lop sided. Those who devote 100% of their energy to work tend to neglect their personal life as well as family life. One important reason for breaking up of families is the imbalance of personal and work life of most working people today. There is therefore a good case for being contented with our wealth without compromising our health and happiness in the process of acquiring it.

Mental health:

When we think about health, we have a tendency to focus mainly on our physical health and not so much on our mental health. Although most work places currently have opportunities for employees to improve their physical health and educational skills in the specific areas of their work, many employers tend to overlook the importance of facilitating and promoting the mental health aspect of each and every worker they employ, with the result that some employees who are unwilling to reveal their true feelings about the type of work they do at work, may find work very stressful. Work places that have aggressive short-term plans to promote their business and products as a winning battle or war that they wage against their competitors, are not conducive to the mental health of workers. The supervisors of such work places could be aggressively stretching their subordinates to meet the deadlines that can make them stressful during and after work.

Selecting efficient workers by interviewing a number of qualified candidates for a position vacancy at work, is important to employers. Similarly, every working person who is planning to spend a good part of her/his life in a work place should look for criteria that s/he would like most in selecting a work place in order that s/he could be doing the work expected passionately. However, this ideal matching of the workers with the work places occurs very rarely.

Food consumption habits as they relate to health:

The stressful work life of working people today may go hand in hand with unhealthy eating habits. Most working people eat on the run; while driving to work they pick up their breakfast in drive-by windows of fast food restaurants. Invariably they tend to eat out in restaurants several times every week simply because they do not have the energy or the enthusiasm to prepare their food themselves coming home tired after work. Even if they prepare their own food, it is simply a matter of microwaving precooked and packaged frozen foods taken out of a freezer. The busy life-style of working parents do not simply allow traditional food preparation at home in a relaxed atmosphere. Traditional homemade food or "grand-ma's food" is becoming a thing of the past. Consequently, food consumption has more or less become something that people do alone in haste than in the company of loved ones with whom they spend time together preparing and enjoying the food together. Ironically, the formal dining areas in most homes stay hardly used or unused except on very rare occasions.

Most people will give good reasons such as saving time for adopting such eating practices and eating behaviors. The main reasons they give are convenience, less time it takes for preparation of foods, ability to find food anytime anywhere and anyway they like, no messy cleaning to do after eating the food, and many other reasons the reader may want to add to the list. This habit of eating out in fast food restaurants and other popular restaurants has permeated globally even in the third world countries today. Consequently, fast food restaurant owners are becoming more and more conscious about healthy foods to cater the needs of the consumer.

How our health during retirement could be our greatest wealth in our health bank accounts:

All the material discussed above show how our health could be the most valuable wealth/asset that we have in our own health bank accounts, and not the money that we have in regular and commercial banks. Even if we have millions of dollars saved in banks, but have compromised our health in the process of acquiring that wealth, it is a very uncomfortable place to be in our retirement age. I have seen many such retirees leading a very painful life and repenting about their past behavior that mainly caused the health problems that they face during their old age.

Bad habits too have a way of accumulating health problems. We may not be able to altogether eliminate health problems that we suffer from in our old age, but we may be able to minimize at least some of the problems if we avoid doing some things that are proven to be harmful to our body. We have a lifetime of opportunity to observe the behavior of people who are around us and learn to avoid bad habits that are detrimental to our health. To cite just one such example, there was an old man known to me who used to brag about his smoking behavior in the following way. "I have two Cadillacs in the two lungs on either side of my chest. That is how much money I would have spent on smoking for 60 years of my life." This statement that he repeated in almost every conversation that I had with him, made me think that the man regretted spending all that money that he wasted on cigarettes. He lived in a rented apartment smoking several packets of cigarettes every day, thereby smoking away his monthly social security check. Since he was mostly sick and coughing heavily, it was obvious that he did not enjoy his last years of his life. He died of lung cancer. My observation was that his wife had to share that misery with him until the day he died.

Unfortunately most people are concerned about their eating habits late in life. They start buying organic foods, all natural foods, chicken farmed with no antibiotics and no added hormones, and cage free, and only consume flesh of animals never fed with animal by-products mostly when they are old. However, the normal tendency of people is to eat anything and everything without even thinking about what they put in their mouths. It is most unlikely that most restaurants will be using meat of animals raised with no antibiotics unless they want to go out of business. The presence of mercury in fish can be a health hazard if the fish eaters do not select the type of fish they eat carefully. Not many people who love eating fish take the trouble to find out how to stay away from consuming fish or fish products with high mercury levels. It is up to the consumers to make the choice of fish with minimum levels of mercury content. Most probably, the restaurant owners may not worry about those details so long as their patrons do not care about it. A useful source showing the mercury content of fish is: http://www.fda.gov/food/foodborneillnesscontaminants/metals/ucm115644.htm

Wealth is a relative concept. It cannot be simply evaluated in terms of monetary value. This is because there could be people who have accumulated much wealth during their life time but are poor in many other ways. The following conversation that I overheard between two elderly men on an elevator highlights this idea. In this conversation one elderly gentleman told the other one, "When I was in graduate school, I could not afford to buy and eat pizza. But now I have all the money in the world, but I cannot eat pizza due to health reasons." Most retirees may be able to relate to this conversation. If we have to spend most of the money that we saved during our prime of life in the hospitals when we are old and retired, we could be indeed poorer than the poorest people on the planet who have no health problems that need costly fixing.

Insight # 7

Wealth is a relative concept. If all the money that we accumulate by jeopardizing our health during the best years of our life, is going to be expended in expensive health procedures that we have to go through at hospitals, it is far better to choose a healthy life style during our younger years that will most probably give us a healthy life in our old age. The best time to think about investing in a healthy life style is when it is not too late for doing that; in other words when we are young.

Chapter Eight

Happiness

If you want to be happy, be ~ Leo Tolstoy

Happiness is a mental or emotional state of well-being characterized by positive or pleasant emotions ranging from contentment to intense joy [Source: http://en.wikipedia.org/wiki/Happiness]. Happiness may mean different things to different people. The goal in this chapter is not to research on the concept of happiness exploring happiness from psychological, philosophical, religious and/or many such other dimensions that happiness could be expressed and/or measured in the human mind and body, but to make some common sense observations as to how a retiree could be happy during her/his retirement years. For this reason the criteria listed below are used to determine the happiness of a retired person:

+ No (or having minimum) financial worries
+ No (or having minimum) unhappiness associated with physical or mental pain
+ No (or having minimum) lonely feelings or depression
+ Sense of being appreciated as a person by the people with whom one lives and shares her/his life with
+ No(or having minimum) encumbrances from family and/or property related issues

- ✦ Being healthy
- ✦ Being satisfied and contented with life at the end of every day as a non-working person (there could be other criteria that the reader may want to add to this list, but you get the idea).

Financial Worries:

Very few people would be working into their 80s today although many can live up to their 90th or rarely 100th year. Taking average retirement age as 65, a person living up to 90 years will most probably live 20-25 years after her/his retirement, nearly 1/3 rd of life as a non-working person, living on a fixed income. Although it is not possible to set a limit to the amount of money that a person may want to save in order to be happy, it is important that a retiree will need to have adequate money to be free from financial worries during her/his retirement years, although one may wonder as to how adequate is adequate. True, different people have different criteria regarding a comfortable life. Having sufficient financial resources to live a comfortable life satisfying the human needs as shown by Maslow in his fundamental needs pyramid,[1] could provide a worry-free retirement to a retiree. As explained in a previous chapter (Chapter 6) careful planning will enable a retiring person to have sufficient income that catches up with the inflation rising every year. It is desirable to account for unexpected emergencies, natural disasters, and health related issues that require additional expenses in case they do happen. Those retirees who saved money during their working years and made investments in growth funds that are safe will have a supply of money that will last as long as they live provided they made careful plans in such a way that they will have a continuous supply of money from their investments as long as they live. It is assumed that those who are disciplined enough to save money for a rainy day will have the same ability to conserve their hard earned money and make that money work for them in their retirement years until the day they die. Also, it is assumed that they will have excess of money to leave behind for their loved ones without ever being a burden on them before or after they die. Therefore not having financial worries is one of the most important components of happiness during retirement. This is one reason as to why most books written on retirement focus mostly on money management aspect of retirement life.[2]

Worries unrelated to having sufficient financial resources:

Nevertheless, being free from financial worries is no guarantee for happiness. There may be many people in this world who are doing financially well but searching for happiness without ever being able to find it. It is a moot point if not finding happiness makes a person an unhappy person. Nevertheless happiness or unhappiness of a person is usually reflected in the overall behavior of a person. Such a state of mind is mostly seen by others around a person than by the person her/himself. For instance, some unhappy people may have a habit of putting up walls around themselves or hardly communicating their feelings with others. Such behavior is mostly known to their close friends or family members. Although it is difficult to generalize on the characteristics that indicate the unhappy state of mind of a person, some unhappy people tend to indulge in food, alcoholic beverages and or narcotics or other similar behavior. They hardly realize that such behavior is only a symptom of the problems that lie underneath their mental status, which can gradually erode their mental and physical health. One of the common causes of retirees' unhappiness unrelated to the amount of wealth and money they have can be their children. Most parents find it extremely difficult to let go of with the children they brought into this world and raised, even after they are grown and long gone and are parents themselves. If movies reflect the society within which they are produced, the infinite and unconditional love and attachment parents do have for their children, is one theme that runs through most societies and cultures – parental love hate conflicting relationship with their grown-up sons and daughters is one most common and popular theme of movies yesterday, today, and most probably tomorrow as well. As reflected in movies produced in most cultures and societies, some parents go to the extent of threatening their children to kill themselves if they do things against their wishes, especially when it comes to their grown-up children finding their own partners in life. Some parents do in fact take such unresolved conflicts to their graves. Some retirees not only worry about their married children's' behavior and life-styles, but also extend those worries to the behavior and life-style of their grandchildren as well. This is a most common characteristic in societies in which traditional family life is disrupted by several divorces that many marriage partners go through in their lifetime and different sets of children they bring along into their newly formed families. Most unprepared retirees can get caught up in such family problems that certainly have a way of eroding their happiness in retirement unless they take precautionary measures to guard themselves against such emotional crises.

Health Issues:

As we all know, our mind has a way of acting upon the physical components of our body consciously, unconsciously, as well as subconsciously. People who believe in fate console themselves by passing on such occurrences to fate, work of the devil, or any other external sources that they are comfortable believing in, but most people hardly realize that the most critical and hidden cause of such health hazards is the work of their own mind. Only those retirees who keep the balance between extreme attachment to and extreme detachment from their children and loved ones would know that they are not severely affected by worries or concerns or depression associated with their children's and or grand children's lives or life patterns.

Not everyone is equipped with a vast knowledge of human psychology and psychiatry - the disciplines that provide the professionals the necessary data, information and knowledge to understand the workings of the human brain/mind. Nevertheless, we as humans owe it to ourselves to make an attempt to study human psychology and psychiatry, at least by reading popular books on these subjects written by experts and practitioners[3].

Not many people today have and live in extended families. Once the children grow up and get married, they go away for good. They have their own problems with their families and with their work. They would not have much time or place for their parents in their busy schedules. In some societies most parents live in their own homes, nursing homes, or in assisted home care facilities. Many well-to-do grown up children pay money to keep their parents in nursing homes or in assisted care facilities until they live. The justification that such grown up sons and daughters provide mostly for keeping their aged parents in nursing homes can be that they are too busy with their work and they do not have the time to take care of their aged parents. Although younger people are uncomfortable talking about the unloving and uncaring attitude they display towards their elderly family members, they somehow convince themselves that they are doing the right thing by moving them to nursing homes or to assisted living facilities when their parents cannot take care of themselves on their own. Most parents who do not want to be a burden to their grown up children, plan on their own to move into a retirement community, and when they cannot do things on their own they move on their own to a nursing home or an assisted living facility. Most importantly, the caring sons and daughters find the best caring nursing homes to suit the retiree life-style of their parents to make them feel at home because they cannot provide such professional care at their own homes and visit them on a regular basis.

Loneliness:

A common denominator of most elderly people, who have already reached the retirement phase of life or are almost getting there, is that they tend to be somewhat lonely. It is most natural that many elderly people do not like the idea of living alone when they are old, perhaps due to their feeling of insecurity. It could also be a function of age as much as many other malfunctions that human body is capable of manifesting during the last stages of human life cycle. Those who would like to read to avoid boredom might not be able to do so due to vision problems, and/or unable to go for a walk due to aches and pains in their body and joints etc.

Some retirees can be depressed by such loneliness. What they see and hear almost every day during their retirement is the passing away of another retiree like her or him in the community. Nevertheless there are ways and means that provide hope and happiness not only to retiring seniors but to almost everyone who would want to be a part of virtual social networks that have been an integral part of human life from the beginning of civilization. The nuclear family was at the center of such social networks that extended to the near and distant relatives, the village, the tribe, the state and the country within which people are a part of. Today's electronic networks facilitated by the Internet is the latest from of such social networks that most people cannot live without even for a day. A few examples of such popular networks in the U.S. are: Facebook, Twitter, LinkedIn, and Google+. But now most other countries have their own popular home-grown social networks.

The underlying reason for the need for people to be a part of such traditional or new social networks is the yearning that most humans have to be connected with others of their own kind for satisfying certain innate bonding needs they may have. For example, people would be satisfied going to church every Sunday and meet with others of their kind and be in communion for at least a few hours that would make them very happy. Some other people would get together and watch a foot-ball or basket-ball game for fun. Others may have parties at home inviting their close friends, have barbeque, eat and drink alcoholic beverages and have a good time.

How to be a happy retiree:

Endless search for happiness is one way not to be happy or contented in life; most people who go after happiness do not realize how happy and contented they could be if they stop seeking for unattainable happiness. Such unattainable happiness can be very similar to a mirage that they see in the happiness of others. Unfortunately, we live in an acquisitive and competitive society that values material possessions, although they may not guarantee happiness and contentment after the pursuit for their acquisition is over.

Many people have a tendency to please others rather than themselves when it comes to everything they do. A good portrayal of this mindset of some people is vividly done by the British TV comedy series Keeping Up Appearances.[4] You do not have to play golf to make your friends happy, if you do not like golf or worse yet, you hate playing golf, because it is not your cup of tea. Unfortunately, there are many people in the world, even those who are retired, who do not have the courage to say no gracefully, to things they do not like to do. In the above mentioned British comedy series long-suffering husband Richard (Clive Swift) gets the brunt of it, with Hyacinth quick to chastise him if he steps out of line ("I don't like you making decisions unilaterally", she tells him). Most retired married couples may have to fit into a similar life-style, if they refuse to understand the real meaning of happiness and contentment a retired life could provide them.

Retirement time for spouses who worked all their life could be a challenge. It is about adjustment to a new way of life. Some people make the adjustment easily but others who are more worried about their "external appearances" rather than how they feel inside themselves about making such appearances, perhaps find adjustment rather difficult. In worst case scenarios of conflict between retiree spouses, such couples may end up seeking psychiatric counsel since they cannot handle the situation by themselves. The one single and most important thing they may forget however is that this is the time of their retirement, and it is the only time in their life they could enjoy life without having to imitate or compete with the Joneses of the external world. One possible way to avoid conflict between couples who worked most of their life, would be to plan a staggered retirement with the employer/s. This arrangement would enable working spouses to phase out of work gradually and at the same time allow them to gradually adjust to the new non-working flexible life with no work stress. This is because some working people would spend the day most productively with stress without which they cannot simply function. In the absence of work demands and stress they may find their retirement life absolutely dull, boring and empty.

Insight # 8

Happiness is a state of mind more than something that one derives from an external source. Some things that are not necessarily tangible like, peace of mind, tranquility, love, satisfaction, contentment, and enlightenment are such experiences of a profound and spiritual nature that most people tend to overlook in this competitive world. Retirement time gives an ideal opportunity for a person to develop internal peace and happiness that do not depend on material possessions.

1. (Source: http://en.wikipedia.org/wiki/Maslow's_hierarchy_of_needs)
2. How to Retire Happy, Wild, and Free, Ernie J. Zelinski, Ten Speed Press, Berkley/Toronto, 2008; How to Retire Happy: the 12 most important decisions you must make before you retire, Stan Hinden, 3rd Edition, 2010; Retirement Bible, Lynn O'Shaoughnessy, Wiley Publishing Inc. 909 Third Avenue, New York, NY 10022,ISBN 0-7645-5245-7,No date
3. People of the Lie: The Hope for Healing Human Evil, M. Scott Peck, M.D, 1998; A World Waiting to Be Born, M. Scott Peck, M.D, 1994; Road Less Traveled, Scott Peck, M.D, 1979.
4. (source: Wikipedia: http://www.bbc.co.uk/comedy/keepingup appearances/.)

Chapter Nine

The Sunset Years

Slow and Steady Wins the Race

We all need to slow down at some point in time in our life. The very last stage of our retirement life is not only the best time of life it is also the best time to slow down. As we advance in age some of us will have our bodily functions slowing down as a natural process of aging while some of us have our brain (and the associated mind and the neurological system) slowing down sooner. There are limits to which even the most advanced scientific and medical technology could provide answers to repair, reverse or remedy this process and related issues involved. For example, the lenses that improve our vision could provide temporary solutions for vision problems as much as our hearing aids could improve our hearing. Same is true of knee replacements, hip replacements and all other body part replacements that are supposed to restore at least some of their original functions. The reconstruction and restoration of teeth as well as the implanting of false teeth and jaw bones is another story altogether. These medical procedures may be absolutely necessary as far as some retirees are concerned. Nevertheless, it is important to understand the benefits as well as the risks of these procedures mainly because some of them could be irreversible. This means, once you make the decision to go ahead with such procedures, you are not able to go back to its original state even if you feel that you were much better off before you went through the procedure. Therefore, it is always better to investigate all your options before you go through any irreversible procedures, especially in your advanced age of retirement.

Since the slowing down of our human body is a natural process, it is best that we are mentally prepared to accept and carefully pre-plan to manage this process. It is best that we accept this slowing down of bodily functions as a natural part of the aging process rather than a sudden event such as a disease that is going to strike us down instantaneously at any moment taking us by surprise. Putting off to plan how to deal with this aging process some time someday in the future would be an unwise thing an aging person could do. This is because time wastes us and not the other way around. The clock will go forward whether we like it or not giving us no guarantees as to what the future will hold for all of us who live on the earth. All humans will go through the aging process and it is in the best interest of every one of us if we share our experiences so that others can benefit from our experiences. Electronic social networks give us a golden opportunity to do that very regularly and from the comfort of our homes today.

Our Body:

The key to resolving any problem, even the most complex ones, is the ability to understand the problem and what causes it before trying to solve it. Even medical professionals will not be able to treat a patient if they do not properly understand the ailment a patient suffers from. Similarly, we should be able to understand the aging process that our bodily functions go through by reading books written on this subject, consulting medical professionals, and other data about our bodily functions that medical professionals depend on for treating various diseases that mostly affect elderly people. It is important to understand that vital statistics of our bodily functions are more important to us when it comes to living a long quality life than to anybody else. It is also important to understand that unlike when we were young our body will have to be supplemented with nutrients to remain healthy. We need to be able to understand and recognize that aging as some medical professionals would have us believe, is not a disease; it is rather a natural process that our body parts go through as they age with time. The key to acquiring such a confidence is the information, knowledge, and wisdom that we should acquire regarding the various functions of our body and mind by reading medical literature and maintaining medical records of our body in a systematic way. Unfortunately, most people who do not take the time and effort to do their own record keeping not only neglect a critical and essential source of understanding of the bodily functions that is very important for managing their health, but also completely passing that responsibility to a third party.

In order that we take control of the process of slowing down of the human body without completely giving the responsibility to a third party, we need to gain a deep understanding of the way our body and mind behave at least during the sunset years of our life. Obviously, some people are in denial of old age whereas others are obsessed with it. These are two potentially harmful extremes. Under normal circumstances, it would most probably be an old age related disease that kills an aged person. Therefore it is essential that we spend at least some time in our advanced years, or ideally before we get symptoms that our bodily functions do not function as they were before, to gain a proper understanding of how our physical system works so that we could keep the balance between being obsessed with illness during old age and/or spend our retirement years in denial of the symptoms of old age. Such a proper understanding of the functions of our body and mind would equip us with risk management techniques that we could use to balance the slowing down process of our body and mind. Even if we do not have to do in-depth studies of various aspects of medical science, we may be able to get a good idea of how our body and mind work by studying readable and reliable literature now mostly available on the Internet and other publications done by medical professionals.

Our Mind:

We are in the habit of consulting and seeing medical professionals for illnesses of our body. But how many people that we know of are not even recognizing that they have a mind too that is equally susceptible to various malfunctions as much as their body? Yes, as long as you have a brain and a neurological system you got to have brain related malfunctions and problems either working for or against you. Even if we assume that most people do know about the critical role their mind plays in their life, how many people would seriously want to study and understand how their brains and neurological systems work? Moreover, how many are willing to consult a counselor or psychiatrist even if they are made to recognize they do have neurological or psychosomatic problems? Normally, it would be the family members, co-workers, subordinates at work and/or others who would regularly deal with them in other social settings that notice such unusual behavior of people.

Similar to studying about human body could help us to understand and prevent the diseases that affect our body, we may stand to gain by studying social psychology, clinical psychology, human psychology, psychiatry, and neurology books and articles written by people who have studied human behavior in theory as well as in practice and written readable material in order that those who do read them could benefit from reading them. As much as medical professionals specializing in most medical specialties are supposed to take at least a few credit hours of psychiatry to understand their patients, other people too in the society can benefit by devoting some time to study and learn how human brain and related neurological system functions. We could then first understand ourselves and then others in the society who we have to live with and deal with on a daily basis in our families, at work or in our daily social interactions. In this regard, Johari Window, a communication model developed by Joseph Luft and Harry Ingram to improve understanding between individuals gives useful information about our inner selves that most of us may stand to benefit from if we take the time to study and learn (http://www.businessballs. com/johariwindowmodel.htm).

Our Soul:

Amazingly, most people in their old age show more attachment to their religious beliefs and ponder about their afterlife. They go to church regularly if they are Christians. They go to Hindu temples for praying and participate in temple activities if they are believers of Hindu religion. They go to Buddhist temples and participate in Buddhist religious activities including listening to sermons delivered by Buddhist priests if they are Buddhists. Irrespective of their age, Mohammedans pray very regularly, go to mosques and pray, and even go on pilgrimage to Mecca when they are old if they could afford to do so. This human behavior most probably indicates that there is a strong relation between old age and spirituality. The strong faith they show in their respective religious beliefs could reflect some sort of comfort and salvation they seek in after life, especially during their advanced age. Some popular religions do propagate the idea of life after death - after life existence. Consequently, most human beings tend to believe that they would most probably be born again in heaven giving them eternal life with no suffering or death, or reborn on the earth depending on the good or bad deeds they did during their life on earth. Followers of eastern religions tend to believe in a migrating soul, *atman* or some kind of magnetic energy that ties up their previous self or consciousness to a new life to be re-born somewhere in the universe. Most existing religious systems appear to provide their respective followers some hope of a continued existence or as in the case of certain religions like Buddhism, non-existence (*nirvana*) if they die with no attachment to worldly life anymore. The lack of a clear and absolute proof of life after death has in a way provided the opportunity for most religious leaders and philosophers to speculate on ideas that most people believe in.

There are others who engage, rather religiously, in physical exercise, yoga, meditation, and praying sessions very regularly. Most retirement communities have facilities for practicing such activities as a part of the services offered to the residents. Intensive and regular engagement in the practice of yoga and meditation by most retirees living in retirement communities or visiting other places, such as places of worship, or in their homes, are indicative of a common search of happiness and tranquility of mind by most retirees as they gradually learn to slow down and move away from a stressful life style. Yes, the time that you spent in pursuing and deriving happiness by the mere pursuit of riches and material possessions passes for most people in their mature age. They see no advantage to material possessions that they could not take with them after their demise. Those who truly understand how their mind works come to attain peace and tranquility by practicing compassion on others as much as on themselves.

It is however interesting that happiness is a temporary feeling that we experience within ourselves. That feeling has a way of rising and falling similar to diminishing returns of satisfaction plotted on a curve. For example, if we become happy watching a football game as most people do, the happiness peaks during the height of the game and declines as the game ends and will reach the lowest point after a while; in other words, the happiness never stays the same. Most activities that give us happiness tend to be similar. We need to repeat the same activity at the same level or even at a higher level to keep us happier. The same is true of food consumption and all other things and activities including sex that we engage ourselves in that bring us pleasurable experiences. However, those who pursue mental happiness by yoga and meditation claim that they constantly maintain and gain a higher level of spiritual attainment somewhat above the previously attained level every time they engage in a yoga or meditation session. This, of course, is debatable and needs to be explored further by those who are interested in attaining spiritual heights by engaging in long-term yoga and meditation practices.

There is a tendency for some human beings to develop spiritual practices and activities that evidently give them peace and tranquility of mind and soul. Most religious saints, poets, social workers, philanthropists, singers, and voluntary workers and even writers belong to this category. Such people do not expect anything in return for the service they provide for the humanity other than the sheer satisfaction and delight they derive from engaging in and delivering their services to mankind. In a way they share what they have earned and learned over a lifetime with humanity as their gift they want to bestow in return upon humanity.

Singing, listening to music, and playing musical instruments are among other activities that help most people including the retirees to be close to their heart and soul as they relate to the nature they are an integral part of. Every culture and religion in the world has an immense wealth of material that almost every person could enjoy and deeply immerse. Hymns of Christian saints such as Amazing Grace are examples that could touch the souls of most human beings not necessarily those who believe in Christianity. The lyrics of this song and the music undoubtedly have a way of transporting the listener to a higher realm of peaceful bliss of the mind that is so close to a mental ecstasy. The words of this song are given at the end of this chapter while the YouTube link allows anyone interested to listen to the song. Country songs of the western world have a similar effect on the singers as well as the listeners giving them a touch of a timeless peaceful bliss that cannot be described in words using natural languages. Most cultures in the world have such creations such as Bharata Natyam, Karnataka Music, and religious *Mantras* or chanting that enable us to detach ourselves from the material world at least during the time when we are immersed in either listening to them or doing such activities ourselves. Links to YouTube examples of Karnatic Music and Buddhist Jayamangala Gatha are provided at the end of the chapter.

Insight # 9

The main purpose of retirement is to be able to relax and enjoy every moment of the remaining life time you will have left after having worked at least two thirds of your life. It you take the scenic route rather than the toll road, you will enjoy the gifts of nature much better for a longer period of time.

Amazing Grace Lyrics:

https://www.youtube.com/watch?v=u4qbmPpfG6s

Amazing grace! How sweet the sound
That saved a wretch like me.
I once was lost, but now am found.
Was blind but now I see.
'Twas grace that taught my heart to fear.
And grace my fears relieved
How precious did that grace appear
The hour I first believed!
Through many dangers,
toils and snares
I have already come;
'Tis grace has brought me safe thus far,
And grace will that lead me home.
We've been there ten thousand years,
Bright shining as the sun,
We've known less days to sing God's praise
Than when we first begun.

Karnataka Music by Sudha Raghunathan
http://www.youtube.com/watch?v=UWOligJE-Es&list=PL4E3817E3560166AF
Jayamangala gatha
http://www.youtube.com/watch?v=lMmfoi0yL6o\

Chapter Ten

True Retirement

Not every runner reaches the finish line

Life can truly be a race that we run against the others as well as against ourselves. We all remember the time when we competed in our elementary, middle and high schools with other class mates. Some of us managed to get to college in this race and some of us fell by the way side. Some of us gained admission to prestigious universities while some of us settled to attend a local community college, local college or a university and got by. Some of us managed to gain admission to reputed universities, and get into prestigious jobs and professions while many others settled for some low-end jobs and settled to get by in life. Who will ever remember or want to remember those who we passed by in our life-long race? Our memory about those who we passed in our life-long run would be very faint at the time we reach our finish line anyway. Mostly, it will always be a faint memory or a forgotten story as far as most people are concerned.

This chapter is for those who managed to reach the finish line of their life and are truly retired. It is assumed that they have found a location of their dreams to spend their retirement (chapter 5), they have sufficient money and minimal financial worries regarding how they would spend for today, tomorrow and as long as they live (chapter 6), they are healthy (chapter 7) and most importantly they are happy and contented (chapter 8).

They have learned to relax, slow down and enjoy every minute of everyday truly appreciating the gifts of nature by taking things easy (chapter 9). This chapter is also for those who are planning to retire and want to reach the finish line some day in the near or distant future, albeit they need to work harder in order to catch up with those who are ahead of them and have slowly but steadily reached the finish line - the real and true retirement goal.

If you imagine that the finish line of life as similar to a mountain top, it is where you are when you are truly retired. You have reached the summit and there is no higher place to which you could climb. You do not want to go down because it would be a waste of time and energy to do so. You do not have to face anymore challenges or hardships in life and this is the time to sit back, relax, and truly enjoy the world in which you spent most of your life having little time to appreciate what it has to offer you while you rushed for work every day to keep food on the table and pay for home mortgages, car liens, and make credit card payments every month during your productive life. Also, this is the time to enjoy the company of those people around you who have time to spend with you without your having to make appointment to see them. All these years you had time just for work, colleagues at work place, and work-related demands that competed for your time with some vacation time that you enjoyed. Now, you have more time to have the vacation you always wanted during the time that you were busy working.

How many people who you know have truly reached this mountain top of retirement? How many people you know who retired truly let go of with their work place? How many retired people you know have truly let go of their projects and desire to cling on to their co-workers looking for another project partnership or consulting work to make some additional income? How many retired people you know are not considering engaging in doing consulting work? "Not many", would most probably be the answer that everyone who reads this will be giving. One major reason for people to continue to work even after their retirement can be their insatiable love for work without which they find life meaningless. Another reason can be the extra money brought in by such work that one may enjoy doing.

An imaginary list of things a retiree would like to do in her/his retirement summit could contain and not limited to the following list:

+ Global travel
+ Recreational activities such as daily work-out, swimming, biking, racket ball, walking etc.
+ Intellectual pursuits including reading, writings, and learning things that you have been wanting to learn
+ Satisfy the interest to learn something new but never had the time to devote to like playing a piano
+ Desire to experiment in cooking and baking your own food
+ Gardening while you can
+ Cruising
+ Fishing
+ Hunting
+ Watching movies that you always wanted to watch and never had the time to watch
+ Ball-room dancing
+ Visiting old friends and family
+ Golfing
+ Mountaineering
+ Meditation
+ Yoga, and last but not least,
+ Learning the basics and practicing playing the stock market for fun

[Reader may add to this list]

As you see, the list may include many things that you want to do sooner than later. For example, if travelling to see the world has been one of your dreams, you need to do it before you reach a time when you find it difficult or unable to travel globally on account of physical/health reasons. One of my dreams has been to visit all the states of United States, visit the tourist attractions, museums, lakes, parks etc. I must plan and make sure that I need to do this at a time when I am still able to drive, if I want to do this on my own. Some folks do hunting, or fishing trips. Certain amount of planning is needed if you were to do such things with other enthusiasts. The whole point being that you need to prioritize things that you plan to do in your list of things to suit your available time when you will be physically capable of doing those things comfortably.

Suppose your best retirement years are 10-25 years, you may be able to do at least 5-10 years of global travel within the first ten years of your golden years of retirement. The idea is to phase out these global trips over 5-10 years extending the enjoyment over a significant period of your retirement years. This is because global travel could present challenges to elderly people. Long trips on planes ranging from 10-15 hours could be physically taxing, exhausting and tiring. Getting used to different time-zones, altitudes, climatic changes, different cultures and societies could be other challenges associated with global travel. Political situations of some foreign countries can be challenging. But of course, most foreign countries have a wealth of cultural and other attractions that will definitely be a plus as well as a life-long memorable experience. I wouldn't trade my one-month coach tour experience in Europe or one-week of Western Caribbean Cruise for anything in the world.

If you do plan to take time traveling, especially in foreign countries, it is most important that you do have fewer encumbrances to worry about such as dogs and cats that depend on you for feeding them and care on a daily basis, and large houses that need to be cared for and maintained in your absence. These are concerns and worries that most retirees should avoid creating for themselves. It would be prudent to live in such a way that your material possessions should not be in the way of your peace of mind, contentment, enjoyment, satisfaction and the joy of life that you deserve at least in your retirement life.

As we all know you may not have enough time to do all the things that you want to do in your list of activities. For example, if reading is one of your interests and you have been putting off reading up on the latest political developments of certain parts of the world, you may take a few years to read up all the material available. The point being you may have to plan your interest with the available time you have. You may not have a single dull moment in your retirement life if you follow a flexible plan that interests you. The most interesting thing about such a plan is that it is your own plan and not your employer's plan or someone else's plan. You will be a happy retiree if you do have a partner (most probably your spouse) who will positively contribute and be a part of your retirement plan. As is always the case, there can be roadblocks on your way. Being prepared for those roadblocks and having other things that you could do instead, will always be an option. For instance, meditation will always become handy to spend time productively without ever having to do anything at all. Going through the techniques of meditation and knowing how to do meditation will always be a useful ally in your hands to tide over stressful situations. There are excellent books and training material on meditation. A search on Google will enable anyone interested on meditation techniques to find useful resources. Here is one such link: http://www.youtube.com/watch?v=bf60XcnpgF8

Obviously, the finish line of retirement is the best time a person has in her/his life. If the purpose of retirement is to enjoy all the things one wanted to do and experience life to the fullest extent, this is the time to do it and have no regrets about not being able to do the things one wanted to do in life. There is a good reason therefore to make hay while the sun shines on you while you are on the retirement mountain top with no other higher place to climb and reach. Therefore, why not take the time to enjoy every minute of your time, including the time that you take a hot bath feeling the water running over your body and the warmth inside you.

Insight # 10

Why do people climb mountains? One obvious answer is that because mountains are there. However, reaching the summit of a mountain, gives one an incredibly awesome experience that cannot be described in words. The satisfaction of reaching a mountain summit is elevated by the hope of being able to be there forever, if possible. Nevertheless there could always be other higher mountains that one may want to climb.

Chapter Eleven

End Of Life Cycle

Nothing is permanent

Human beings enter the world and ultimately depart from it alone. It is very unfortunate that they do not have a clear idea or vision into their future. Perhaps it could be nature's way of keeping the humans wondering and guessing forever and being hopeful for a healthy and longer life. The future is presented to them like a mystery so that they do not have to worry about the day they die as in the case of those who are terminally ill or sentenced to death and are doomed to die (killed) on a specific day. Some people belonging to certain cultures believe that astrologers could predict their future accurately by making calculations based on how a person's date and time of birth is related to the formation of the galaxy of stars at the time their birth takes place. Nevertheless the reality is that humans can only predict the future events by making some educated guess using probability as their guiding principle. The truth of the matter, however, is that in all probability the retirees who reached the finish line of life and enjoyed the golden years of their life would also reach the end of their life slowly but surely.

All good things have to end some day. Life begins and life ends, and that is how the life cycle works. When systems reach obsolescence, new ones take their place, like old trees give way to new ones or large computers are replaced by smart phones. The same thing happens with all animals including the humans. This is the nature of nature. But humans have a hard time accepting the end of their life as real. Some humans seek eternity even after their death as the Pharos of Egypt did. This could be one plausible reason as to why most religions make us humans believe in life after death, reborn in heaven, hell or any other blissful place at the end of our life on earth. The pharaohs who constructed pyramids in which they preserved their dead bodies in Egypt apparently believed that their souls would be transported to the distant stars of the galaxy. Accordingly, those pyramids were supposed to have been constructed in perfect alignment with the distant stars. Same was true of belief systems of people who constructed the Mayan Civilization of South America.

In today's prosperous and thriving civilizations, most ordinary people would rather avoid thinking or talking about the subject of death or life after death or would want to postpone thinking about it to a later date. Most people would rather change the subject if it ever came up in a discussion. This may be because they think that it is unproductive for us to allow our minds to wander about such depressing and negative thoughts. The life on earth is generally perceived as a wonderful and pleasurable thing. Not many people would like to associate with pessimistic people who would talk, think, or worry about death. Positive thinking is encouraged even when the worst thing on earth happens to people. This is one reason that death is considered an occasion to celebrate and not lament about in the western world. Such a positive approach helps those who live on the earth to leave it in a happy state of mind when they die.

Nevertheless, most oriental religions, like Buddhism provide a very pessimistic idea about human life. Such religions although pessimistic, are very down-to-earth and very pragmatic about life on earth. Those religions originated in geographical regions at a time when human life literally involved utmost suffering on earth and emancipation from such suffering was considered as bliss (attainment of *nirvana or nothingness*). At the time when Buddhism originated in the 6th century B.C in north India, there was internal strife among many kingdoms involving the killing of humans by other humans, wide spread diseases, poverty and hunger. Death was a common sight and it was accepted as a very normal part of life. The acceptance of such teachings based on a pessimistic view of life on earth by the vast majority of laymen as well as others who renounced lay life and became Buddhist ascetics in large numbers during the life time of the Buddha indicates that life on earth during that time in those geographical regions must have been a very unpleasant experience. Unlike Hindu or Christian clergy, no Buddhist priest conducted or attended marriage ceremonies at the time when Buddhism was widely accepted as a religion in India, south Asia and south East Asia; rather they only conducted and attended funeral rites and rituals. It is very normal even today to witness dead bodies burned in open air in public places in such societies. It is mostly in the developed part of the world that disposal of dead bodies is performed by special purpose institutions, such as funeral homes and church burial grounds where the burial or cremations are performed in close groups performing funeral rituals in accordance with the last wishes of the deceased and the family members of the deceased person.

The Reality:

In reality we need to look at the last few years of our retirement life in the light of the above discussion. All of us whether we are retirees or not need to understand and accept the reality that either you or your spouse will be gone sooner or later. This is of course, if both you and your spouse reached the finish line of retirement and lived as a retired couple at least a good part of your life together. To deny this reality and not being able to accept it is unrealistic. Statistically, women live longer than men. The average life expectancy for men versus women in the U.S. according to a list of life expectancy of men versus women published in 2013 is 77.4 for men to 82.2 for women (Source:http://en.wikipedia.org/wiki/List_of_countries_by_life_expectancy). The sooner retired couples come to terms with the fact and realization that one of them, most probably the female partner, will be missing the other spouse for good is better for them so that they could deal with that event realistically and calmly at the time they have to face it in real life. Such an understanding of reality may open up a good opportunity for them not only to communicate with their soul partners about that dreadful event dispassionately but also to treat their partners in a very kind and caring manner as long as they live as life partners. This may of course, be somewhat different in the case of single people who may have had a single life all their life, but such cases of retirees are growing in numbers these days.

When one of the spouses dies, the other surviving spouse can be very lonely and perhaps be miserable and depressed under normal circumstances. Knowing about it ahead of time will be extremely helpful in order that steps could be taken to get over the impact of devastating emotions that arise at a critical time in last few years of retirement life. Normally, when one spouse spends all the time and energy on the other sick spouse for a long time, the death of the sick spouse and the resulting impact would completely devastate the surviving spouse and s/he too would pass away after a short period of time. In such a situation an environmental change could perhaps help a surviving spouse to continue on with life.

Living in a retirement community among like-minded and/or with the same age or older people having common interests could be one way to deal with loneliness that occurs by the loss of one partner by the other. Finding a suitable retirement community takes time and should be done well before it becomes a pressing and an acute need. Getting used to a community takes time. Making acquaintances and friends in a retirement community usually takes longer. Although there is no guarantee that living with such a community of friends will ensure your happiness after the death of a loved one, there is at least some hope that the surviving spouse won't feel all alone, depressed and feeling miserable that s/he is all by her/his self in the world without the company of the loved one who had been there for her/him most of her/his life time.

In traditional societies the function of such care for the elderly was the responsibility of the grown up children. This is still the case in certain societies of the orient. However, such traditional care given by the grown up children would not always be ideally suitable and would not be a tremendous source of satisfaction to the old parents and grandparents. This is because such an arrangement would not always work in the best interest of both the young and the old people who would be living together as an extended family.

In the western world however home care, assisted living, and hospice care are available for elderly people who have Medicare, supplemental medical insurance, and/or long-term-care insurance. These all cost money, pre-planning and payments made regularly over long periods of time; therefore such arrangements need to be planned well ahead (ideally before a person reached 60 years of age) before long-term illnesses occur at all. In addition to these various sorts of insurance policies protecting old people against illnesses, most people who are retired in the western world have social security benefits - monthly payments made by the government depending on their work and earning history. In the oriental world, unfortunately, most elderly people will have to depend on their own savings, government pensions (if they worked for the government), provident funds, and other investments, and/or their grown up children for taking care of them during their very last few years of life.

Except tragic accidents or things of that nature, the most probable cause of an old person's death would be a disease. Most fatal diseases are heart related, lung related, brain related or even stomach related to name a few. Some diseases like cancer in various parts of the body bring lingering death while others such as massive heart attacks could take the life away immediately. Strokes could debilitate a person's life significantly and kill the person over a long period of time. There are other debilitating conditions like blindness due to old age, hearing loss, dementia associated with Alzheimer's disease or neurological conditions associated with Parkinson's disease. Such diseases could bring disaster for both the person afflicted with the disease as well as for her/his loved ones. In a way those people who die in sleep are more fortunate than others who die after submitting themselves to all kinds of treatment in various hospitals over long periods of time. For instance, those who suffer from the worst kind of leukemia or such diseases having to go through chemotherapy and blood transfusions several times or until they continue to breathe do suffer untold misery in their hope for survival. Such human suffering could perhaps be one good reason for terminating the life of those who suffer at their request. Such mercy killing or assisted death is however not an option or available in almost all the countries. The only four places that openly and legally authorize active assistance in terminating the life of patients are: 1) Switzerland (1941), Oregon (1997), Belgium (2002), and Netherlands (2002).

Considering all these things that could happen to an old person as s/he grows older, retirees may have to make decisions regarding the last few years of life well ahead of time while their mental faculties are still alert and functioning properly. The usual tendency of most people is to leave it open ended like those who die without leaving behind a last will or trust. This may be a bad idea. It is always a good thing to know what can happen next before it happens as a surprise. This is because all surprises are not good and wonderful surprises. If you know what is waiting to happen and is ahead of you, then you could plan and be prepared for it before it happens to you. Managing uncertainty may be very difficult but there are times when we have to take careful stock of the situation and manage even the most uncertain things in our life. The end of the golden age of retirement is one such place that we have to manage with care.

Managing from the grave:

It is far better to do some kind of planning of the aftermath of your death during the time you are capable of doing so, while you are mentally and physically active. Some people either postpone or altogether neglect this responsibility and thereby leave certain important and critical issues unresolved for their survivors. Following are some of the important things that a retiree should be planning during the last phase of her/his retirement. The reader may have additional ideas and thoughts:

1. Leaving behind a last will and or a revocable trust that gives all the details of all the assets and liabilities of the deceased person. Such a document should be invaluable for determining the last wishes of the deceased person regarding the distribution of the material possessions s/he had. A revocable trust or Will would enable smooth transition of real estate titles etc. that eliminates probate procedures by the court/legal system. It is very important that such legal documents have to be prepared by attorneys qualified to do so; such legal documents need to be updated periodically. This is crucial to avoid unpleasant feeling among family members after the death of a person who, they thought would leave behind substantial amount of wealth as inheritance. The worst possible situation resulting from an elderly retiree, who leaves behind grown up children and grand children without leaving behind a Will or a trust, is that the family members having to go to court to settle inheritance problems that may drag over a long period time. The author has witnessed many families breaking apart and members of families becoming bitter enemies on account of family feuds involving inheritance.

2. Many retirees during the last few years of their life have good intentions on bequeathing some part of their wealth to charitable purposes. Some examples are: setting up college scholarship funds, making funds available for research on certain diseases like cancer; donations to religious, medical, and other charitable institutions as one time or on continuing basis; establishing community service centers in one's memory; charitable offerings given to the poor people annually etc. But, unless actions have been taken to ensure that these intensions are carried out and followed through according to the wishes of the person before her/his demise, those good intentions however good they are, will not materialize. Pre-planning to execute those intentions is therefore as important as pre-planning the death and the aftermath of a retiree discussed in the next section.

Pre-planning the aftermath of one's demise:

Funerals are for the living, not for the dead. Some people want to give the best and most memorable and glamorous funeral for the deceased person. But it is more important to give the best and most comfortable life for a person before s/he dies.

Unlike in the case of a wedding, there is no time to do a whole lot of planning when a person suddenly and unexpectedly dies. If the death was not expected as is the case of most deaths, there could most probably be a chaotic and confusing situation among the family members of the decesed person. In cases where the family members are spread all over the world, a death of a family member could present many difficult situations if the funeral arrangements were not planned ahead of time. The family members under such circumstance will have their hands full in planning for the funeral of the deceased person, in addition to making travel arrangements and at the same time dealing with the grieving process.

Some of the immediate needs in this process are 1) registering the death and obtaining the death certificate. There will be data and information needed for this process 2) planning the funeral; decisions will have to be made if it is a burial, cremation etc. 3) depending on religious affiliations of the deceased person, this could be a simple or a very complex process. The bereaving process of some cultures could go on for long periods of time. Complex religious rites and rituals could create unforeseen difficulties for the family members. 4) Finding a suitable funeral home and deciding upon the immediate and future expenses involving the funeral could be difficult for people who are inexperienced in handling funerals that happen once in a life time of people. For example, a casket could cost from $3000 to $ 10,000 to fit the needs and expectations of the family members of the deceased person. There is hardly any time to shop around or to make the best decisions for buying a suitable death ceremony package for a person by the immediate members of the family who would most probably be struggling to purchase an air ticket to attend the funeral. For this reason, most elderly people make arrangements in their last will and give their consent to the hospital authorities to cremate their body (the most inexpensive and simple way of dealing with the dead body) if they thought that they may most probably die in a hospital. A quick look at the obituaries of the day published in the daily news paper is one way of finding out how many of the deceased persons whose obituaries appear on that date died in the local hospital.

The above discussion makes it clear that it is far better for a person in the last stage of her/his life to pre-plan her/his funeral in the way s/he wanted it so that her/his death would not present problems to the family members. Some people for example, go to the extent of providing details regarding the type of burial stone they want to be placed above their grave and the inscriptions to be carved on the stone, and the hymns to be sung at the funeral ceremony etc. Some people apparently want an elaborate funeral ceremony, while others want something very simple. There are others who do not do anything and consequently die leaving the responsibility entirely in the hands of the family, or friends as the case may be. But it is very important if a funeral is planned rather than not planned at all. It is more important from the point of view of a retiree to die happily than unhappily and plan for such a happy and graceful ending of a memorable retired life.

Insight # 11

The most valuable gift a retiree could pass on to her/his loved ones is a last Will and/or Trust that clearly details all material possessions s/he possessed and how those should be distributed among her/his loved ones and or for charitable purposes.

Epilogue

A walk in the park could be an eye opener

This book on retirement though brief, put together by collecting daily journals written over a life time is similar to a quick walk-through of my thoughts on retirement long before and after my own retirement. Some ideas expressed in the book, especially in the concluding chapters may be viewed as negative thoughts by some readers. However, some truths are unpalatable and there is no way that we could camouflage them without seriously distorting the underlying substance.

A walk in the park simile was chosen in the epilogue because it is a silent time that I mostly spend in reflecting upon my own self without being distracted by many other worldly affairs that affect our minds and souls in the mornings listening to daily news. It is a time similar to being engaged in deep meditation while walking at the same time. It is also a time that I spend connecting me with the nature, the wind that blows across me, the trees and the birds that I see as I walk, and the fresh smell of the earth that fills me in the morning.

The insights given at the end of each chapter are my own thoughts that I developed over the years as I reflected upon my own retirement from work. I hope they provide valuable ideas towards formulating a plan for the retirement life from the very beginning of any career most people engage in, during the most productive years of life. They are presented to the reader in order that they formulate their own ideas as they contemplate on retirement. This is my own way of ending my retirement by sharing my own ideas with the rest of the world in my sunset years of life.

Glossary

James A. Autry, The Spirit of Retirement: Creating a Life and Personal Growth, Prima Publishing, 2002

Elizabeth Armstrong (edited by), America's 100 Best Places to Retire: the only guide you need to today's top retirement towns, Vacation Publications, Houston, 2003

Jan Cullinane and Cathy Fitzgerald, The New Retirement: The Ultimate Guide to The Rest Of Your Life, St. Martin's Press, 2004

Morley D. Glicken and Brian Haas, A simple Guide to Retirement: How to Make Retirement Work For You, An Imprint of ABC-CLIO, 2009

Robert P. Delamontagne, The Retiring Mind : How to Make the Psychological Transition to Retirement, Synergy Books

Marika and Howard Stone, Too Young to Retire, 101 Ways to Start the Rest of Your Life, A Plume Book, 2004

Lynn O'Shaoughnessy, Retirement Bible, Wiley Publishing Inc.

Nancy K. Schlossberg, Revitalizing Retirement, Reshaping Your Identity, Relationships, and Purpose American Psychological Association, 2009

Ed Slott, The Retirement Savings Time Bomb: And How to Defuse It, Penguin Books, 2012 Edition

Jan Warner & Jan Collins, Next Steps : A Practical Guide to Planning For The Best Half Of Your Life, Quill Driver Books, 2009

Ernie J. Zelinnski., How To Retire Happy, Wild, and Free, Retirement Wisdom That You Won't Get From Your Financial Advisor, Ten Speed Press, 2008.

www.ingramcontent.com/pod-product-compliance
Lightning Source LLC
Chambersburg PA
CBHW070546290526
45790CB00002B/593